I0754884

THE INNER PASSAGE

VIRGINIA MCGEE RICHARDS

AN UNTOLD STORY OF
BLACK RESISTANCE ALONG
A SOUTHERN WATERWAY

INTRODUCTION BY IMANI PERRY
FOREWORD BY JAMES ESTRIN

THE MIT PRESS
CAMBRIDGE, MASSACHUSETTS
LONDON, ENGLAND

The MIT Press
Massachusetts Institute of Technology
77 Massachusetts Avenue
Cambridge, MA 02139
mitpress.mit.edu

The MIT Press would like to thank the anonymous peer reviewers who provided comments on drafts of this book. The generous work of academic experts is essential for establishing the authority and quality of our publications. We acknowledge with gratitude the contributions of these otherwise uncredited readers.

The author is grateful for the expertise that Caleb Cain Marcus of Luminosity Lab and Yasuyo Iguchi of the MIT Press both brought to realizing the design of the book.

This book was set in Adobe Garamond, Grand Central, and Scala Sans by the MIT Press. Printed and bound in China.

Library of Congress Cataloging-in-Publication Data is available.

ISBN: 978-0-262-05171-2

10 9 8 7 6 5 4 3 2 1

EU Authorised Representative: Easy Access System Europe, Mustamäe tee 50, 10621

Tallinn, Estonia | Email: gpsr.requests@easproject.com

CONTENTS

FOREWORD

ON THE PHOTOGRAPHS

JAMES ESTRIN

In the South Carolina Lowcountry, the boundaries between past and present are permeable. The air is thick with humidity and the echoes of the brutal violence against enslaved Africans brought there in the seventeenth and eighteenth centuries. Traces of the Inner Passage waterway that these enslaved people were forced to construct still exist, but their names and stories are lost to time. However, through years of painstaking research, Virginia McGee Richards has uncovered rare documents, maps, and records that help piece together the outlines of this largely forgotten story.

Richards swam in the waterway and walked along its banks for days on end, searching for any clues that could lead her to a better understanding of this tragic saga. Ultimately, she realized that the heart of her story is beyond the reach of the documents she found. It is within the land itself, within the muddy marshes and in the movements of the water. Every day, the tide surges five to seven feet, flooding the wetlands. Every day, the tide retreats, returning the land to where it was the day before, transformed but unchanged.

The truth, she found, also lives in the centuries-old oak "witness trees" that overheard whispers in myriad African dialects, English commands shouted by overseers, the many languages of the native peoples, and the French, Spanish, and Portuguese of the traders passing by in small boats. These trees also saw the enslaved people who dug the waterways use them to escape from their oppressors.

But how does one unlock such a story? Richards turned toward photography, a medium perceived as a prisoner of time, good at recording events and landscapes since its inception but incapable of portraying pre-photography history. She wrestled with how to make images that would evoke and honor the lives of the enslaved people in the Lowcountry. She strived to create photos that would both transcend and incorporate the epochs of the story.

While photography can now be made and distributed in an instant with digital technology, Richards chose the much slower nineteenth-century wet-plate collodion process to make exposures of more than ten seconds with a ninety-year-old Graflex Universal Camera on eight-by-ten-inch glass and tin plates. On a good day, working from before sunrise until after sunset, she was able to make four or five images. Because the collodion process requires the plates to be coated, exposed, and developed all within ten to fifteen minutes, Richards prepared the plates and processed the photographs in the fields of South Carolina with a portable darkroom in the back of a 2010 red Toyota Tacoma.

The resulting black-and-white photographs are ethereal and go far beyond capturing historical facts to reveal visceral truths. Because of the wet-plate collodion process, the viewer experiences the images as ancient. Yet the photographs feel immediate and are shockingly precise in their details. Today, descendants of the Inner Passage waterway live near each other along the shores of the Lowcountry, on the South Carolina Sea Islands, and within the city of Charleston. Richards' poetic portraits of these Americans reveal the enduring effects that these seventeenth-century events have had on more than a dozen generations.

In *The Inner Passage*, Richards' images are rich and resonant in their tonality and operatic in their scope. Her work comes out of the great Southern storytelling tradition honed on porches and around fireplaces that produced writers such as William Faulkner, Carson McCullers, Toni Morrison, Tennessee Williams, Richard Wright, and Flannery O'Connor. Because of Richards' devotion to unearthing the story of the people who built the Inner Passage, this too is now a tale that can and should be retold on porches, around fireplaces, and throughout the nation.

INTRODUCTION

ALONG THIS WAY: LIVING HISTORY IN VIRGINIA RICHARDS' LOWCOUNTRY PHOTOGRAPHY

IMANI PERRY

I pause to hear a racketing triumph of cicadas Setting life's pitch . . . [1]
—Derek Walcott

In Gullah tradition, mourners stand at cemetery gates to ask permission of their ancestors before they enter. It is one of many African-descended rituals in which respect for the departed shapes how we move today. In the Lowcountry, such respect depends on recognition of both suffering and valor. The first time I set foot in the region, my spirit felt rapt, at attention. I was responding to the beauty, of course: the flora and the historic architecture. But the intensity of my response most certainly had to do with the sense of haunting in the place—so much happened here, many things that would tear your heart out and some things that would make your spirit soar—as well as with the straight-shouldered confidence with which so many of the locals bore the weight of that history. Long before, as a very young child, I'd heard the syncopated singing of Bessie Jones and the Sea Island Singers, carriers of Gullah Geechee heritage; I'd even danced alongside the famous culture-bearer; but it was another matter altogether to hear that sound inside a praise house, the clapping backed by the chirping cicadas, or with light ricocheting off a cobalt blue bottle–decorated tree. In this place, even speech is a song, as everyday phrases are heavy with parables for living. The encounters I had over many years in Charleston, Savannah, St. Helena, St. Simons, Johns Island have always been deeply spiritual experiences. They demand a contemplation of the concept of reverence. What and who do we revere, and why? There are so many parts of the past that demand respect: the humans, of course, especially the ones whose labor and land were stolen, lives cut short or made rough by greed. And the flora and earth, too, that have survived and fight back with lushness despite frequent misuse or exhaustion. But there is also

1 Derek Walcott, "Midsummer XVII," in *Midsummer* (New York: Farrar Straus & Giroux, 1984).

history, that term of art for the deliberately remembered past. History has its uses, ones which today are so often in competition with each other, reflecting different values and commitments.

And that brings me to the work of Virginia Richards. She has chosen an ethical form of reverence, one that depends on truth telling and intimacy with both people and nature, and which takes shape in the form of art and story. Richards and I first met several years ago when I was commissioned to write a short article to accompany her photographs of coastal South Carolina. She is at once a fine art and documentary photographer and a historian. But that list feels like it doesn't quite cohere enough. Richards offers a testimony for how the past lives inside the land, and inside us more broadly. In 2024, I traveled explicitly to meet with her, to learn about her method of recording past and present in image, and thereby to gain a deeper understanding of this storied region and the nation itself. It was a trip to witness the living.

Richards picked me up before the sun was fully up. A few minutes after 6 a.m. we were on Charleston Harbor looking to meet a young man named Kyle. Charleston looks like any other picturesque harbor town in the United States. The boats are small to mid-sized and gleaming white. I note their difference from Richards' photograph of an 1840s canoe, worn and richly brown. The way the world has changed over the centuries—with planes and telecommunications—makes it easy to arrive in many cities and feel an immediate sense of familiarity. The docks often look alike, the boats too; in towns across the Americas and across the world, there are familiar stores and signs, even for the throngs of tourists from far-flung places. Still, this is a very particular place. Colonial South Carolina was rice country. The plantations in the Lowcountry depended upon the knowledge and skills of enslaved Senegambian people, as one of Richards' collaborators, groundbreaking historian Peter Wood, famously demonstrates in his classic text *Black Majority: Race, Rice, and Rebellion in South Carolina, 1670–1740.*[2] Other crops would be important as well, such as indigo, cotton, and tobacco, but none as significant as "Carolina gold" (i.e., rice). From the first decades of the 1700s to the Civil War era, it was the leading crop.

The British were in contemporary Barbados first, before they arrived in what is South Carolina seeking more land. The Lowcountry is characterized both by a specific history and by its biodiverse ecology full of salt marshes and winding waterways. Enslaved West Africans from coastal areas had greater familiarity with this type of environment than the Europeans. This was famously true when it came to rice, but it was also the case with fishing and the use of botanicals for healing and nourishment. Economically, the colony

2 Peter H. Wood, *Black Majority: Race, Rice, and Rebellion in South Carolina, 1670–1740*, 50th anniversary edition (New York: W. W. Norton, 2024).

depended upon the Africans for survival. Culturally, their importance would shape the region.

In the early colonial period, however, there were also Indigenous people enslaved in South Carolina. And while the settlers were British, the Spanish had preceded them by generations. The various populations, including representatives of competing empires both trying to get a foothold and a bounty in the land, and African and Indigenous peoples, both trying to obtain or maintain freedom, together shaped history and the very land on which it unfolded.

Though the sun was just recently up on this July morning, it was already sleeveless weather. Thankfully, we beat not only the blazing sun but the inevitable boat traffic to come after 9 a.m. Charleston is a popular tourist destination filled with elegant shops and the bustle of restaurants and hotels, but just beyond, or better yet, beneath that veneer, out there, is an old-world complexity. Though Kyle drove us out onto the water in his modern boat, our surroundings were quiet enough for us to imagine the past with relative ease. Venturing out, we traveled slowly along the Ashley River and crossed under the large and modern James Island Expressway Bridge. Perhaps this was the speed at which the 1840s canoe Richards photographed would have traveled? Though we were not moving quickly, very soon the city was far enough behind us to seem absent. The nonspecific dock had morphed into a particular landscape. Grand houses with private docks sat on each side of us, as we traveled the water. Our craft, voices, waves, and birds made the only sounds. Occasionally a fin poked up from the water.

We drifted through Wappoo and Elliott's Cut. "Cut" is a term of art on the Carolina coast. It refers to a place where a straight waterway has been built through one that was once winding. These "cuts" were fashioned in response to the desires of Southern planters. They found it arduous to bring their crops to market—in Charleston or to farther-flung places—because they had to skirt the coast through Atlantic waters or attempt to travel across interior shallow and meandering marshes and creeks. They decided to make the latter navigable.

In 1712, the South Carolina colonial legislature passed "An Additional Act to the Several Acts for Making and Repairing of Highways."[3] The legislation included the following explicit intentions: "The head of Wappoo Creek going into the Stono, be cut and made sufficiently wide, or that a new creek more convenient be cut from the head of Wappoo into the Stono at the discretion of the commissioners." The act went on to specify that "the creek . . . shall be made ten feet wide and six deep" and that it was to be dug "at the

3 David J. McCord, ed., *The Statutes at Large of South Carolina: Acts Relating to Roads, Bridges, and Ferries (1703–1838), with an Appendix Containing the Militia Acts prior to 1794* (Columbia, SC: A. S. Johnston Press, 1841), 26–29.

usual charge and labor of all male persons . . . living from New cut to the head of Stono River to the plantation of Colonel Robert Gibbes."[4] The legislative words, as was often the case when it came to colonial slavery, excluded the cruder and even harrowing aspect of the endeavor. These hand-excavated channels were built by enslaved people using arms, backs, and minds while facing the hazards of water, under the burning Southern sun. These men "shoveled mud through malarial swamps, while battling snakes and alligators in intense heat," as Richards explains. The Wappoo Creek was deepened in order to better connect it to the Stono River. Riding along the seamless water, we see the effects of their early labor that has been added to with more sophisticated tools over generations. Although I know the story, I am surprised. I'd expected the scent, color, and tangles of cypress trees and marshy earth. But to create the cut, the primeval trees had been chopped. And the blending of salt and fresh water meant they wouldn't return.

4 McCord, *The Statutes at Large of South Carolina*, 26.

Even before the creation of the cuts in the early eighteenth century, Black freedom seekers had traveled along these waterways against the will of their masters. They were lured by the promise of emancipation once they reached Spanish land, and so they braved the swamps. For example, as Jane Landers writes in *Black Society in Spanish Florida*, "In 1687 Florida's governor, Diego de Quiroga, reported to Spain that eight men, two women, and a nursing child had escaped from Carolina to St. Augustine in a stolen canoe and were requesting baptism into the 'True Faith.'"[5] The promise of emancipation wasn't a matter of Spanish benevolence. Instead, it reflected negotiations of territory and empire. The Spanish interest in offering freedom to the enslaved was not an opposition to the institution but rather an effort to prevent the British encroachment into their territories further west and south. Once the runaways reached Florida, they were officially granted their freedom in exchange for converting to Catholicism. These Black freedpeople and their descendants were able to live in Florida in relative liberty until the nineteenth century, when Florida was annexed by the United States.

5 Jane Landers, *Black Society in Spanish Florida* (Champaign: University of Illinois Press, 1999), 24–25; citing J. G. Dunlop, "William Dunlop's Mission to St. Augustine in 1698," *South Carolina Historical and Genealogical Magazine* (January 1933): 26, 27.

Despite how thoroughly documented this history has been for the past five decades, it still challenges conventional American understandings of the history of US slavery, which tends to focus exclusively on the British trajectory and center its narrative on the Black Belt or the Gulf Coast. It also demands a reframing of how we think of enslaved people. As Peter Wood demonstrates, colonial Black South Carolinians were not mere chattel; they were what he terms "Atlantic actors."[6] This means they were people navigating a complex political and economic landscape with intelligence and courage. To be treated as chattel did not mean they would or could be reduced to such. And though

6 Wood, *Black Majority*, 145.

forced to do debilitating labor for the planter class, they also worked for their own vision of freedom.

Richards points to a land mass before us. "That," she says, "is Church Flats." It is where St. Paul's Parish Church (1707) was once located, along with a parsonage. Travelers who stopped at Church Flats, a midway point between the Sea Islands and Charleston, shared local news, conducted business, and socialized. It also was a way station for people waiting out the tide when it flowed against their intended destination. In time, it would shift direction.[7]

7 Kimberly Pyszka, Maureen Hays, and Kalen McNabb, "Small but Convenient? An Update on the St. Paul's Parsonage, Hollywood, South Carolina," *Church Archeology* 18 (2017): 46, 47.

Richards explains to me that the parsonage house only survived for eight years, as it was burned in July 1715 during the Yamasee War. That consequential war essentially ended the enslavement of Indigenous people in South Carolina. The Yamasee Confederation was organized to protect their land and people from colonial domination. In April 1715, they attacked St. Helena's Parish, and in July they killed seventy parishioners at St. Paul's and burned seventy houses in the area along with the parsonage.[8] The event was momentous enough that it threatened the stability of the South Carolina colony. Historians argue that it was the colony's alliance with the Cherokee that allowed the state to survive.

8 "The Stono Preserve's Changing Landscape: St. Paul's Parish," Lowcountry Digital History Initiative (LDHI), accessed April 28, 2025, https://ldhi.library.cofc.edu/exhibits/show/stono-preserves-landscape/landscape-of-religion/stpauls-parish.

The church itself stood after the raid, but no pastor was assigned to it. Ultimately, it was dismantled and the bricks were carried elsewhere to build another church. However, the area kept the name Church Flats until the late nineteenth century. Dixie Plantation took its place. Shifting tides, changing names, history layered on the land.

It is not as though this history is visible, of course. But as I look at the pristine green stretch, I am reminded that the land holds tragic stories and often survives them despite the greed of humans. This lush environment captured imaginations—for some, it offered the prospect of expanding empires and growing wealth at the cost of human life; for others, knowledge of the land gave them ways to regain it despite theft of their land, or to regain life despite theft of their labor; and for others still, navigating its places of subterfuge became a way to find home far away from their ancestral homes in Africa. If one reads runaway ads of the early eighteenth century, there are numerous accounts of Black people living in the swamps along the marshes in maroon communities, and some living with Indigenous people.

The instability of the Carolina colony, the presence of Indigenous nations, and Spanish colonialism are all important contextual elements for a historic event that took place a couple of miles west of Church Flats, on the Stono River, in 1739: the Stono Rebellion.

The revolt began on Sunday, September 9, 1739. Led by an Angolan man named Jemmy, armed and shouting, the insurgents met at the Stono River in St. Paul's Parish. They stole more guns, killed white folks, and continued south through the night, until they reached a farm near the Jacksonboro ferry on the banks of the South Edisto River.[9] Soon thereafter, their rebellion was squashed. But importantly, it was not an isolated event. Other rebellions preceded it: On St. John in 1733, in the Bahamas in 1734, on Guadeloupe in 1737, and in Jamaica, earlier in the year in 1739. These insurrectionists were part of a dispersed hemispheric community of people who reacted against the injustice of their condition from various locations. One account, offered by an unnamed author but whom Peter Wood has argued was Governor Oglethorpe of Georgia, demonstrated how well their contemporaries understood the insurrectionists as Atlantic actors: "Amongst the Negroe [sic] slaves there are a people brought from the Kingdom of Angola in Africa, many of these speak Portugueze [sic] (which Language is as near Spanish as Scotch is to English) by reason that the Portugueze [sic] have considerable settlement and the Jesuits have a Mission and School in that Kington mand [sic] Many Thousands of the Negroes there profess the Roman Catholic religion."[10] They'd not only arrived in the colony with an essential body of knowledge with respect to rice cultivation and farming more generally, but many were also multilingual and politically sophisticated.

9 Wood, *Black Majority*, 276.

10 "An Account of the Negroe Insurrection in South Carolina, October, 1739," in *Stono: Documenting and Interpreting a Southern Slave Revolt*, ed. Mark Smith (Columbia: University of South Carolina Press, 2006), 14.

The South Carolina colony acted decisively in response to the Stono Rebellion. The 1740 Negro Act, which was passed in response, required planters to conduct more surveillance of enslaved people. It also limited their right of emancipation—in an effort to keep the free Black population small—and it enforced a duty on the importation of new slaves in an attempt to slow down the growth of the Black population. Furthermore, it limited the modest freedoms of enslaved people, like the right to buy liquor and carry arms, and mandated corporal punishment for running away. In the aftermath of the rebellion, just as the waterways were streamlined, so too was the institution of slavery.[11] Despite these efforts, the African population continued to grow, and by 1775, almost sixty percent of the population was Black. Slavery was simply too lucrative to be contained by law.

11 Wood, *Black Majority*, 283–286.

"Today, Church Flats, once known as Dixie Plantation, is called Stono Preserve," Richards explains. Under the authority of the College of Charleston, it is being restored to support its natural ecosystems and will function as a pedagogical site. As a photographer, Richards is an educator too, but she is asking us to see more than biodiversity in the living environment—to see its history as well. I realize this as I pass places that once were, and notice what has and has not been remembered. As a Black woman, I travel on these waters freely rather than as a fugitive, and, without question, that reality owes a debt to Jemmy and his allies. Though they were defeated, freedom dreams persisted. The evidence of such dreams is sometimes quite clear, and other times fugitive. Richards is recording it all.

At this point, we could have traveled south along the Dawho River and Watts Cut to reach the South Edisto River, and I have a vision of that waterway in my mind's eye from having seen Richards' photographs. But instead, we angled toward Wadmalaw Island, where we disembarked. Richards was going to take me to see the life on land.

Wadmalaw is small, ten miles by six, and sits to the southwest of Johns Island. We walked through ankle-deep water up the bank to the place near where, in 1666, Captain Robert Sandford and his crew landed on Wadmalaw with the intention of establishing "Carolina."[12] The cicadas are loud and the water is warm in my shoes. The air is redolent. It is a green-scented place—indicating that the earth is mightier than human habits here. We sit on the porch of a mighty home, a former plantation belonging to friends of hers. There, we eat peaches and pore over maps where she shows me the progression of the cuts over the years, and the way the names of places changed or remained the same.

We tossed peach pits to the land before walking around. Trees covered by Spanish moss surrounded us. Richards and I walked among them as she described how the wet-plate process allowed her to capture their texture and depth. The Spanish moss here is so pervasive that it covers not only the live oaks but even the saw palmettos and bushes. Each strand of Spanish moss has a single stem that branches out into curving and slender leaves. It is rootless but chains together, propagating through the winds, and gets caught in the snares of reaching branches. The potential metaphors seem endless. I'll share just one. The people of the coast were displaced repeatedly, slavery and colonialism are fueled by displacement, moved about by the winds of commerce and yet bound together. But also, like the oaks, they rooted themselves in the land. And the oaks are fantastic. Richards refers to them as "witness trees." Over the course of two hundred years, Richards writes, these trees "absorbed the sight of angled elbows against the land, backs bent, as hundreds of men sacrificed their lives to carve canals from the swamp. The trees stood over Black men burrowing so deeply into the gray marsh that they disappeared into it." These oaks are the only creatures still alive today that witnessed these sights, and in the quiet of their presence we hear their testimony. They tell us of the people who sheltered in their branches or behind their thick brown trunks, breathing heavily, wet with sweat, dew on the grass and moisture in the air.

12 Robert Sandford, "A Relation of a Voyage on the Coast of the Province of Carolina, Formerly Called Florida in the Continent of North America to Port Royal in the North Lat: of 32 Deg: begun 14th June, 1666," in *The Genesis of South Carolina, 1562–1670*, ed. Hon. William A. Courtenay (Columbia, SC: The State Company Press, 1907), 51–54.

To make images that capture the past and present at once, Richards uses a mid-nineteenth-century photo process called wet-plate collodion. It requires both time and care and results in detailed and layered images filled with shadows and depth. At each location, she constructs a portable darkroom box where she prepares a piece of glass by coating it in collodion mixed with chemicals that produce a light-sensitive liquid mixture. The glass is then placed in the camera and exposed. Finally, the plate is returned to the black box to be developed before printing. "My hope," she writes, "is that images can convey a landscape scarred with secrets. . . . Planting seasons, river baptisms, torture, prayers, African dialects, poverty, massacres, lynchings. The land remembers but cannot speak. By documenting the Inner Passage, I want to give the land a voice."

We got in Richards' car and drove through Wadmalaw. Along the way we stopped at a cabin which appeared to have once been a slave cabin, though it seemed to have been occupied long after. Stepping on the porch, we found the motley material culture of a place once vital but now abandoned. There was a joggling board—a Lowcountry seat used as a gentle swing—an old horse's saddle, and a rocking chair. Though it looked as if no one had been there for many years, it also seemed as if whoever had last lived there was in the midst of living when they left. If, as it appeared, this cabin had survived use after slavery, that wouldn't be unusual. Many folks remained on the land, working on farms, and gigging for crabs, fishing, and netting other seafood.

The place is thick with spirit. Richards is observant. Though a diligent researcher, she has none of the dispassionate affect of academics. Her take is multisensory, including feeling. "Do you feel it?" she asks me at one point. And I do. Both in person and in the photos. And indeed, spirit and emotion are evident in Richards' photography. In a photograph taken near Jacksonboro, South Carolina, we see the ruins of the Pon Pon Chapel of Ease, erected in 1725 and replaced in brick in 1754. That church was then destroyed by fire in 1801 and came to be known as Burnt Church, a name that was classically Southern—idiosyncratic and matter-of-fact. It carried that designation until it was rebuilt around 1822; it was mysteriously destroyed again in 1832. For nearly two centuries, the ruins have remained.

So do the praise houses, simple wooden structures built by and for enslaved Black people. The church was the first institution of Black American life, before enslaved people had property or even a right to domesticity. Praise houses served as places of religious intercession, exhortation, and devotion, and also as sites for conflict resolution, political development, and education. The contrast between the rubble of the Pon Pon Chapel of Ease and the carefully maintained praise houses makes me think of two words: "ruins" and "ruint." Ruins are detritus. "Ruint," a Southern vernacular term, is a reference to having been destroyed by disgrace and, often, sexual violence. To be ruint was one of the many forms of violence experienced by the enslaved. The praise house served as a place for spirit cleansing and new life. Many of these structures are still being sustained with tender attention today. Others are left in a state of abandonment. Both tell the tale.

Richards' images of trees and architecture tell the history but so too does her portraiture. She captures the faces of multigenerational descendants of this history from across the color line. With the widespread displacement of Indigenous people, this became a land of Black and white people, whose faces bear traces of shared lineage and that of Indigenous people too. Beyond genealogy, theirs is an intertwined culture. In particular, the legacy of the past Black majority is evident in Gullah Geechee people, whose material culture, language, and foodways are everywhere in South Carolina and in the Lowcountry regions of Georgia—even in the places where the actual people are not present.

The Gullah Geechee people are descended from Senegambians, of course, but also from people from all along coastal West Africa. On the coastal islands, slaveholders were often absent or were present in very small numbers, allowing for the blend of West African culture in the Americas to develop there in a way that sustained many features of West African life, including linguistic structures, spiritual rituals, and farming and foodways. In addition to rice, their expertise in growing sweet potatoes, okra, watermelon, and other crops fed South Carolinians in ways inherited from West Africa. South Carolina "red rice" is virtually identical to West African "Jollof rice," for example. Richards' portrait of Benjamin "B. J." Dennis is a way of documenting this tradition. Chef Dennis is known as one of the most important contemporary representatives of Gullah Geechee cuisine. A Charleston native, Dennis cooks local and seasonal food, often hosting large gatherings outdoors in traditional fashion. He also travels throughout the Caribbean and West Africa, tracing the cultural legacies that provided the foundation for Lowcountry cooking. His work, like Richards', revives the interconnected histories of New World peoples across the southeastern United States and the Caribbean. In his portrait, the depth and assurance that has always struck me about this place is evident. It is rootedness without bombast.

The same is true of Herb Frazier, a lauded South Carolinian who most recently has served as the senior projects editor at the *Charleston City Paper*. He's the author of a number of books that record Gullah Geechee culture and history, and trace the transatlantic connections between South Carolina and West Africa. One book in particular comes to mind when I gaze at his portrait: *Sleeping with the Ancestors: How I Followed the Footprints of Slavery*, co-written with Joseph McGill Jr., founder of the Slave Dwelling Project. In the book, McGill describes his project of choosing to sleep in the remaining places where enslaved people once lived. As McGill writes, "In these places they experienced the full range of human emotion while they adapted to slavery and their forced estrangement from Africa. These structures are some of the most visible artifacts of slavery and, as such, should be viewed as sacred spaces."[13] I think back to the abandoned cabin. So much life, complex life had been there, so much that wasn't documented formally. And yet people like Frazier and Dennis testify to tradition that is, to my mind, at least as good as documentation. Frazier described how on a visit to West Africa, "I walked where captured Africans were held before they were shipped to Charleston and other American seaports. Then I connected my childhood memories with an African source and the ancestors who brought their customs to America, giving rise to Gullah Geechee people along coastal South and North Carolina, Georgia, and parts of Northern Florida."[14] And "Africa was evident in the African-style rice dishes we ate, the African words we spoke like tote, okra, cooter, and biddy, the syncopated hand claps in church. . . . The face of Africa morphed into the faces of Black women who strolled gracefully along city streets with heavy loads balanced with dignity on their heads."[15]

13 Joseph McGill Jr. and Herb Frazier, *Sleeping with the Ancestors: How I Followed the Footprints of Slavery* (New York: Grand Central Publishing, 2023), Kindle location 174.

14 McGill and Frazier, *Sleeping with the Ancestors*, Kindle location 72.

15 McGill and Frazier, *Sleeping with the Ancestors*, Kindle location 85.

Richards and I got into her car to begin the land route back to Charleston. It stayed quiet; Wadmalaw is not heavily populated. We stopped at another dock, where Cherry Point Seafood is sited. We were greeted by Micah LaRoche, a ruddy, easy-smiling white man with white hair and a warm spirit. LaRoche owns one thousand feet of dock on Wadmalaw. Though it is a lot of property, this is not an easy trade. Costs are high, and private outfits like his have to compete with large commercial fisheries. Richards introduced me to LaRoche and he hugged my shoulder and smiled, looking almost identical to the image Richards had captured of him. Remarkably, the redness of his face, the warmth and worry of his eyes, windswept hair, hunched shoulders, in living color, are fully communicated in textured black-and-white, but what Richards also reveals is how he is a son of this land, generations into this place. After a brief chat, we walked inside his business while he drove off to do some business. Richards bought a bag of shrimp weighed out by a personable teenager wearing a baseball cap, his long curls hanging down. The slick floor and industrial architecture repeated yet another truth: human beings have always used ingenuity to manage our relationship to the environment. Old architectures juxtaposed against new ones are a matter of development, but they also reflect changing relations of power. The big commercial fisheries threaten to displace operations like Cherry Point and, with them, human-to-human relationships. The history is difficult, but the only adequate confrontation with it requires human encounter with people differently situated, Black, other, owners, workers, across the lines of gender, sexuality, culture, and with that serious interrogation of how we might honor the past without being held hostage to it. I think of my cousin in Alabama who wears a T-shirt that reads "Respect the locals" that is produced by a clothing company in Philadelphia where I live, and I cut off that final "s." Respecting the local is, I think, a requirement for environmental and social ethics. And I take that to be what Richards is getting at with these deeply resonant and layered images and why this very particular place can and should have relevance for us all. What happened here, what happens here, reflects so much of who we are but also what we might be if we trained our gazes with care.

On the wall of Cherry Point Seafood, there are a series of watercolor paintings. I notice the nuance of the blues in each piece. Within a few moments, the painter walks in. He is Sherman Mack, a local fisherman turned artist who is capturing history through his own lens, as Richards is. He tells us that he has been doing house portraits recently. I imagine the houses we saw riding out on the water. These impressive edifices delighted my eyes with their beauty, but they hurt my heart too. The descendants of those who built and worked these places are largely left dispossessed of their bounty. They live more humbly, by and large. Mack's house portraits could very well be capturing a place his, or my, ancestors built and worked. But art itself, like language and story and a connection to the land and an ethos of maintaining tradition, is a bounty of its own. Mack's presence is genteel, elegant in his graciousness, yet steely. I am again astonished at how faithful Richards' artful rendering of his face is: his eyes filled with both wisdom and wonder, a man who is at once lean, beautiful, and deep. They say the photographer paints with light. Richards captures the sunlight in his gaze.

Back in the car, we drive over Esau Jenkins Bridge. I always teach Jenkins' story in my classes about the civil rights movement. He was born on Johns Island in 1910. A farmer, Jenkins and his wife used the bounty from their land to send children from the Sea Islands to Charleston, where they were able to access more formal education than they could on the islands, and eventually he was integral to the establishment of the first high school on Johns Island. During the civil rights movement, in collaboration with educator Septima Clark, he was a leader in the establishment of citizenship schools, which combined the demand for suffrage rights and desegregation with civics education. Theirs was one of the most significant initiatives during the movement. This is not just a place of haunting memories, but also of hard-earned triumphs. Richards drops me off at my hotel, but as I walk the streets of Charleston, and long after, I keep thinking about what I've seen.

With the taste of salt in the air and the slight refuge from the heat under a sprawling live oak, the land that once held so many captive inspires with its betrayal of boundaries—and so do its children. The ancestors just keep pushing. "You feel their presence," Richards said. Indeed, we do.

PORTFOLIO OF PHOTOGRAPHIC PLATES

WITNESS TREE, WADMALAW ISLAND
Live oak tree, estimated to be over 300 years old, grows beside New Cut canal on the Inner Passage.

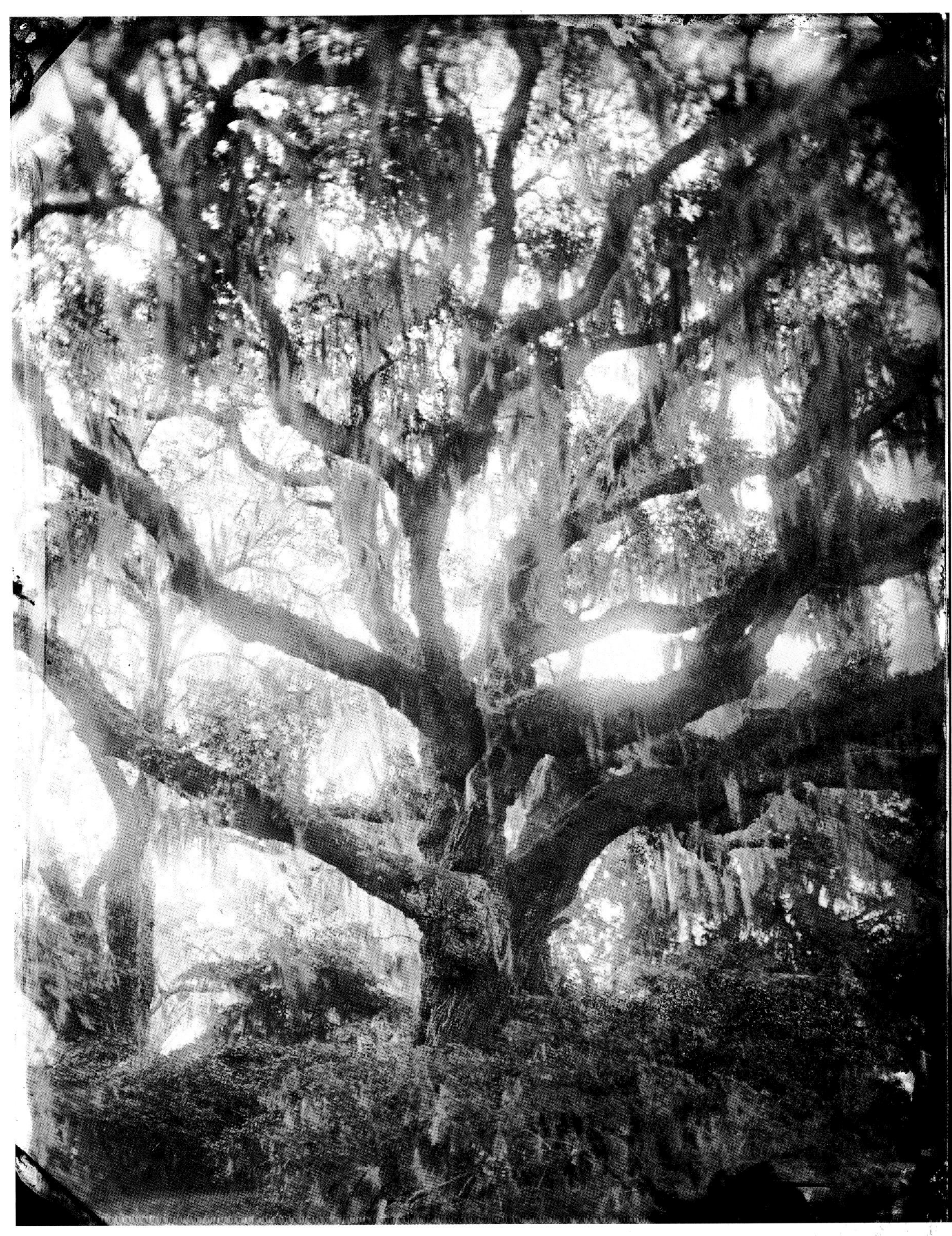

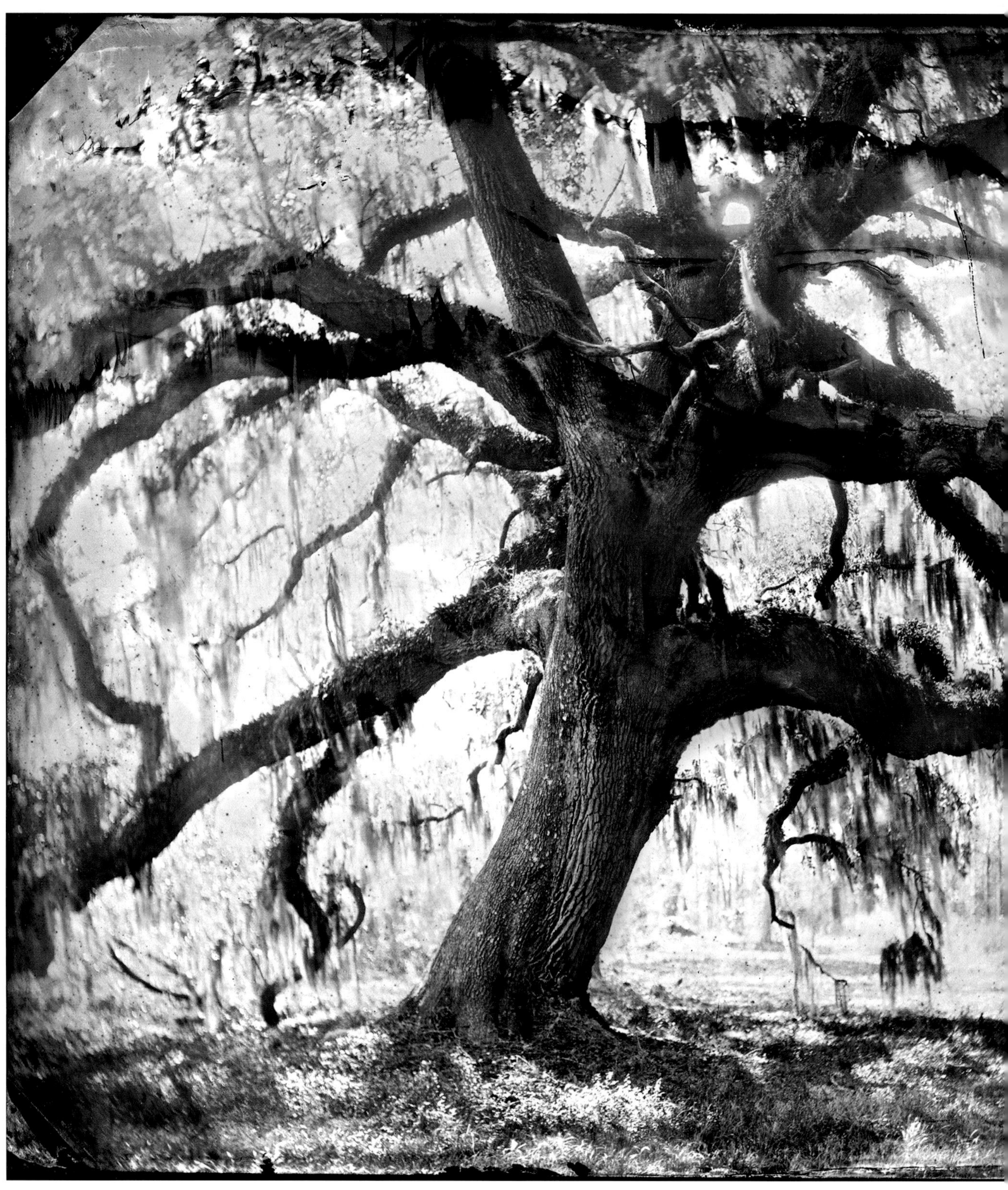

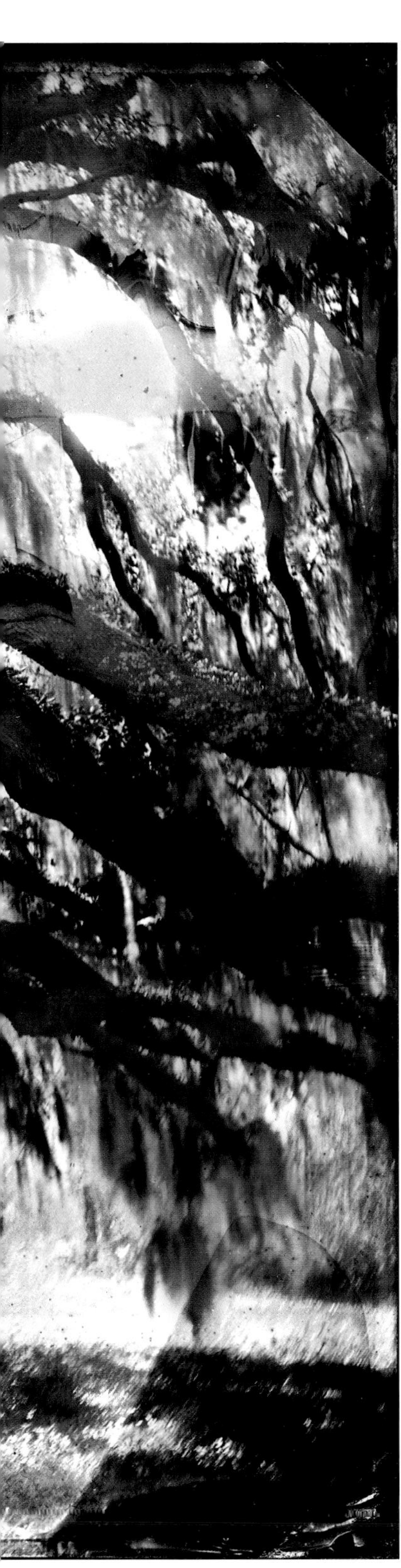

LIVE OAK TREE, COLLETON COUNTY
Witness tree beside former rice fields on the Combahee River. The agricultural fields were abandoned after the Civil War ended, but many of the earthen dikes and rice rows remain visible in the fields at low tide.

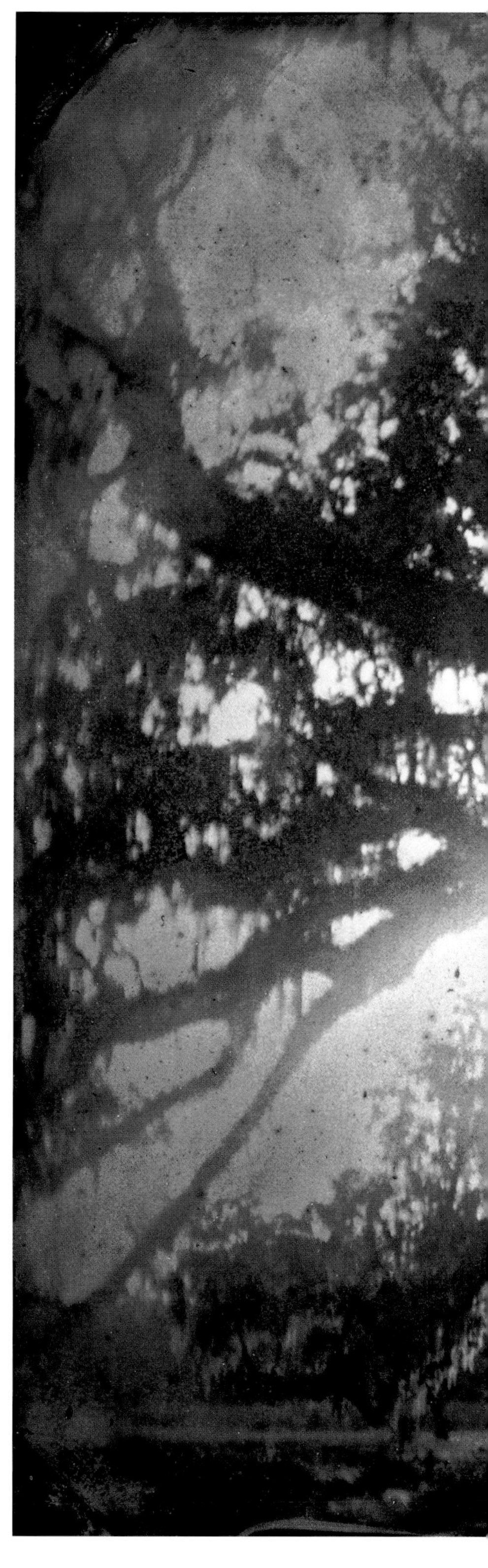

WITNESS TREE, MIDDLEBURG PLANTATION
This ancient live oak stands over land where twelve slave dwellings were located at Middleburg Plantation. The cabins are no longer standing.

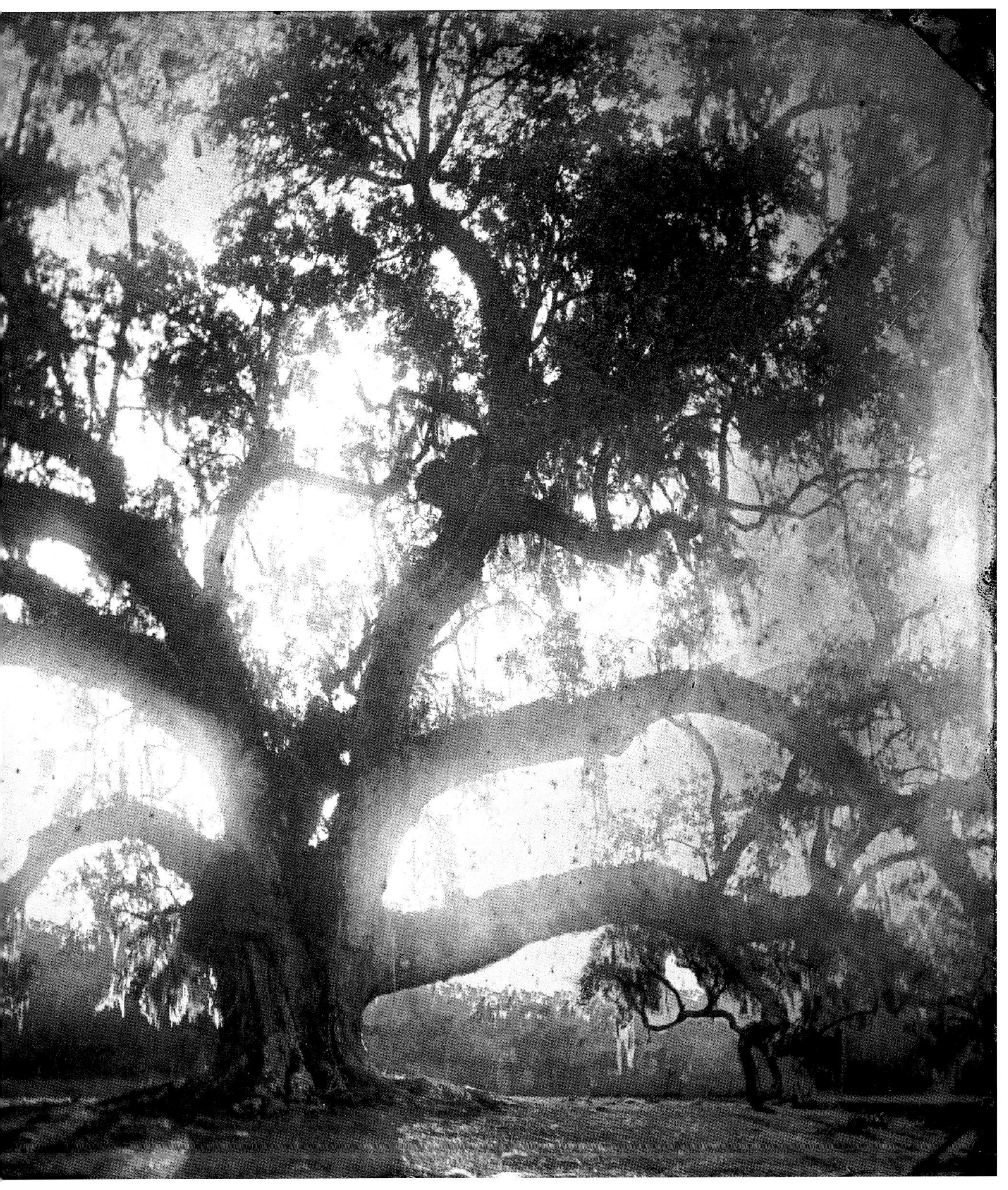

JOHNO CREEK, COLLETON COUNTY
Planters living on farms alongside this narrow freshwater creek loaded rice barrels on boats that traveled over forty miles on the Inner Passage to Charleston.

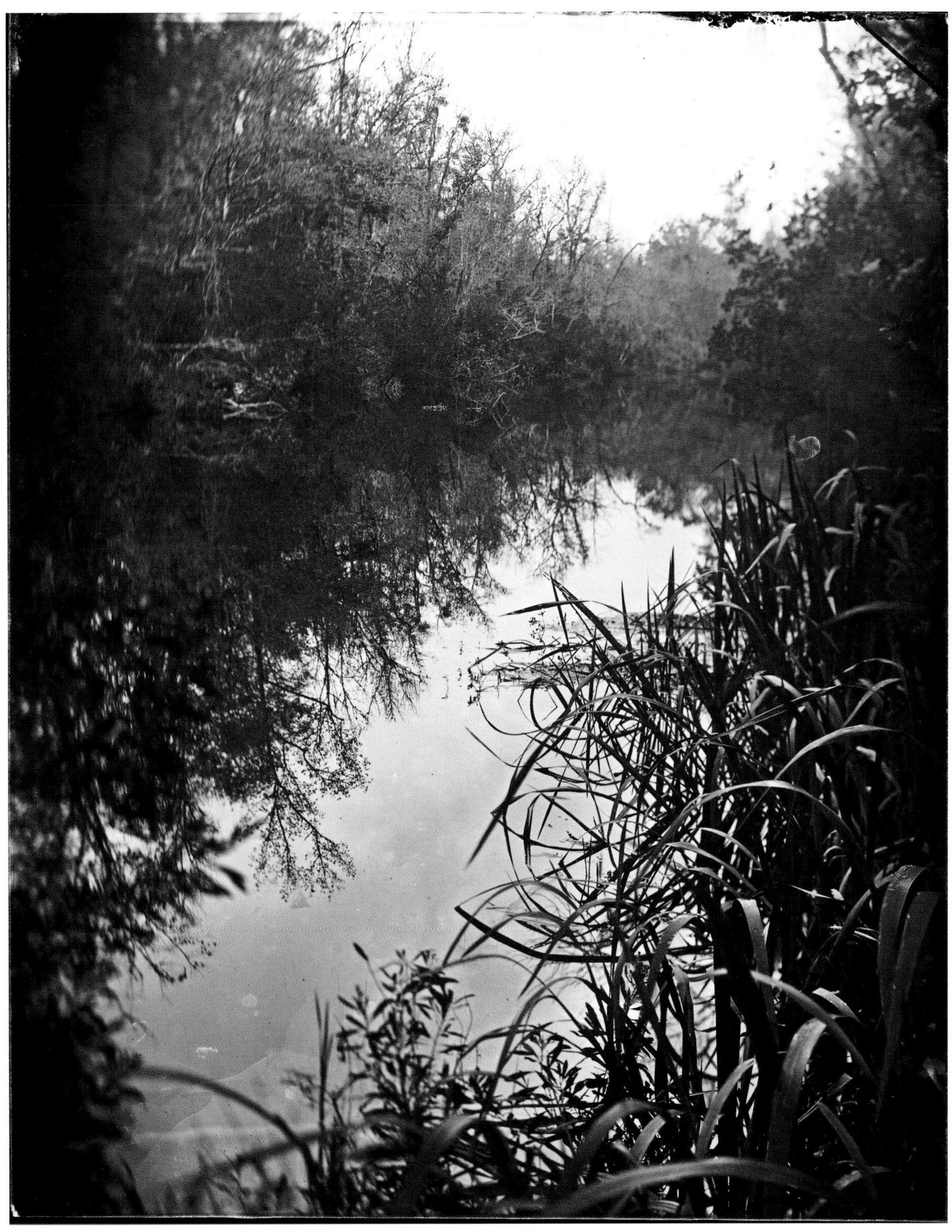

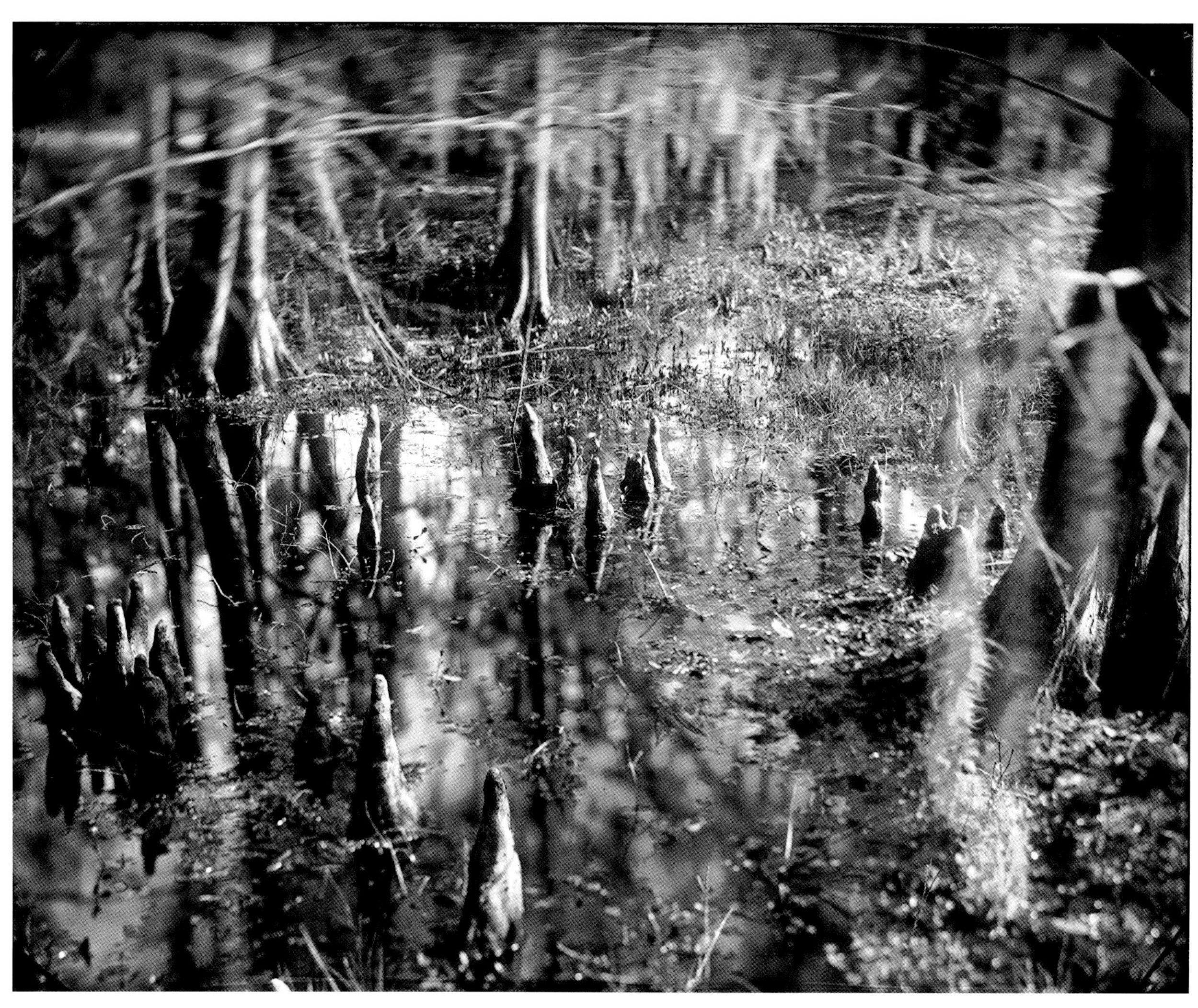

CYPRESS KNEES, COLLETON COUNTY
When European settlers arrived in Carolina in the late 1600s, primeval trees covered acres of coastal land. Whole cypress forests were felled at New Cut to create channels for the Inner Passage.

BOAT CANAL TO THE ASHEPOO RIVER
During the antebellum era, enslaved laborers hand-dug a water channel to transport rice grown on Cockfield Plantation to Charleston. This canal is now filled with trees and impassable.

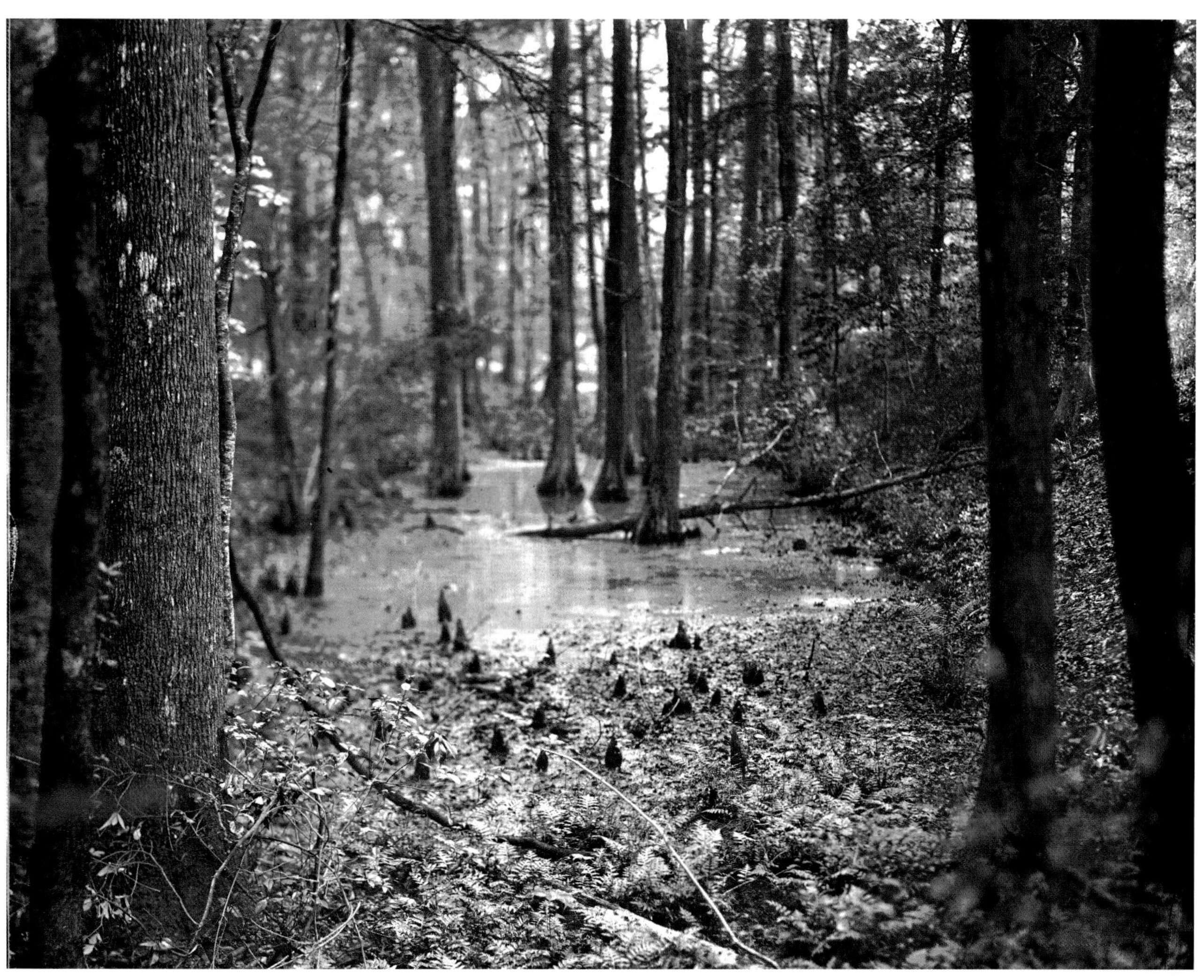

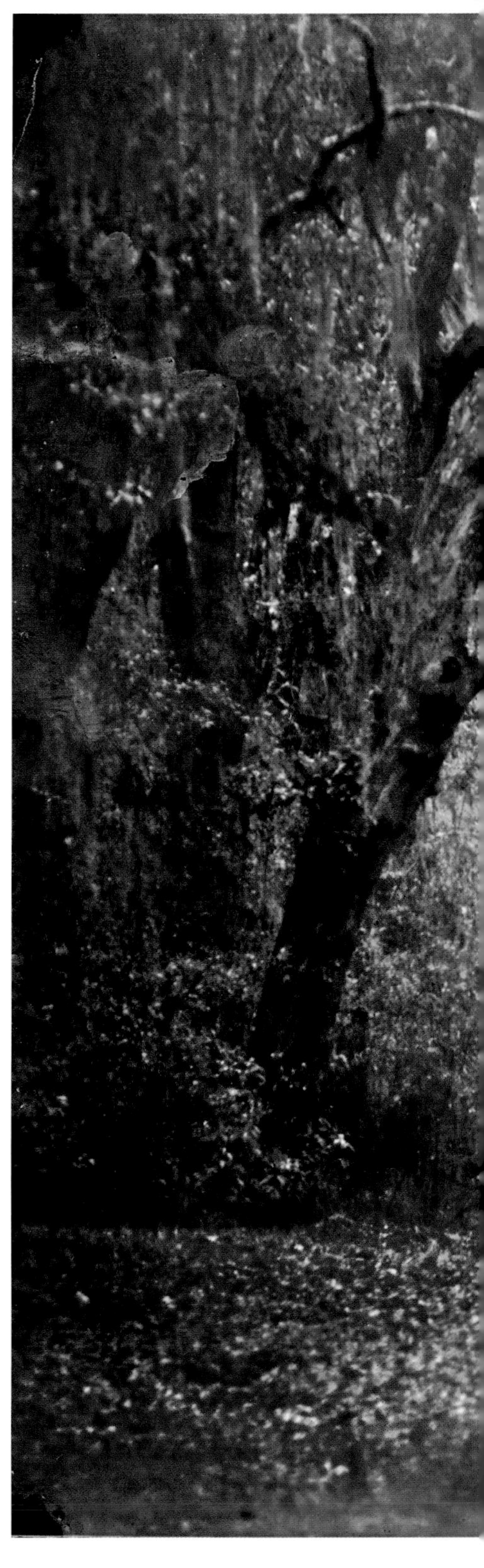

ROAD TO NEW CUT, WADMALAW ISLAND
Colonial travelers left buttons, pipes, and other artifacts found along the road to the New Cut ferry.

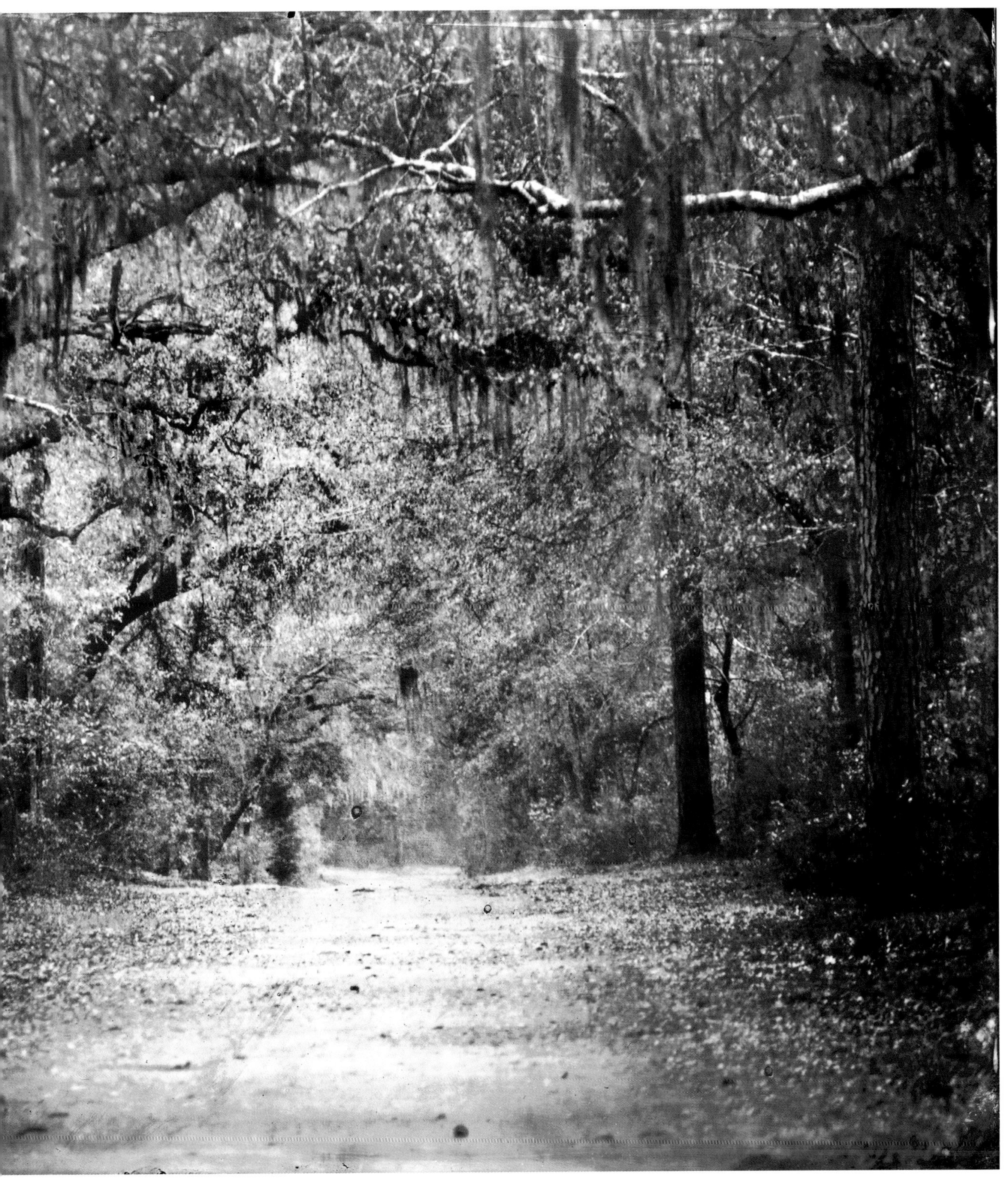

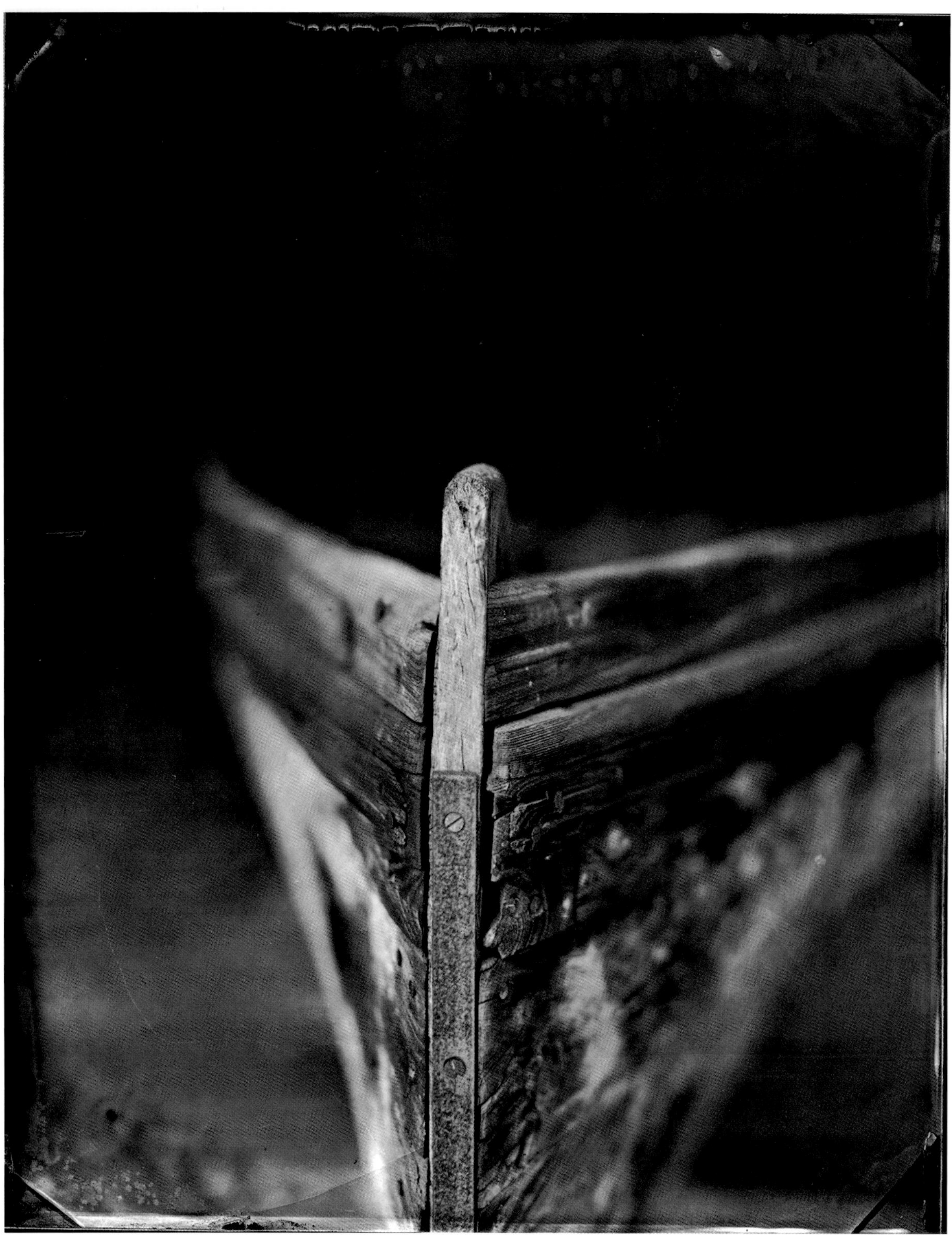

PLANTATION BOAT, CIRCA 1840s
Bessie, a plantation barge with a hull from a single cypress log, was built in the 1800s on a rice plantation and used for travel on the Inner Passage waterway.

BARRED WINDOW, HYDE PARK PLANTATION
Amos, a carpenter who was enslaved, built a house in 1743 that still stands at Hyde Park Plantation on the Cooper River. Hyde Park Plantation shipped rice to Charleston on boats traveling on the Inner Passage.

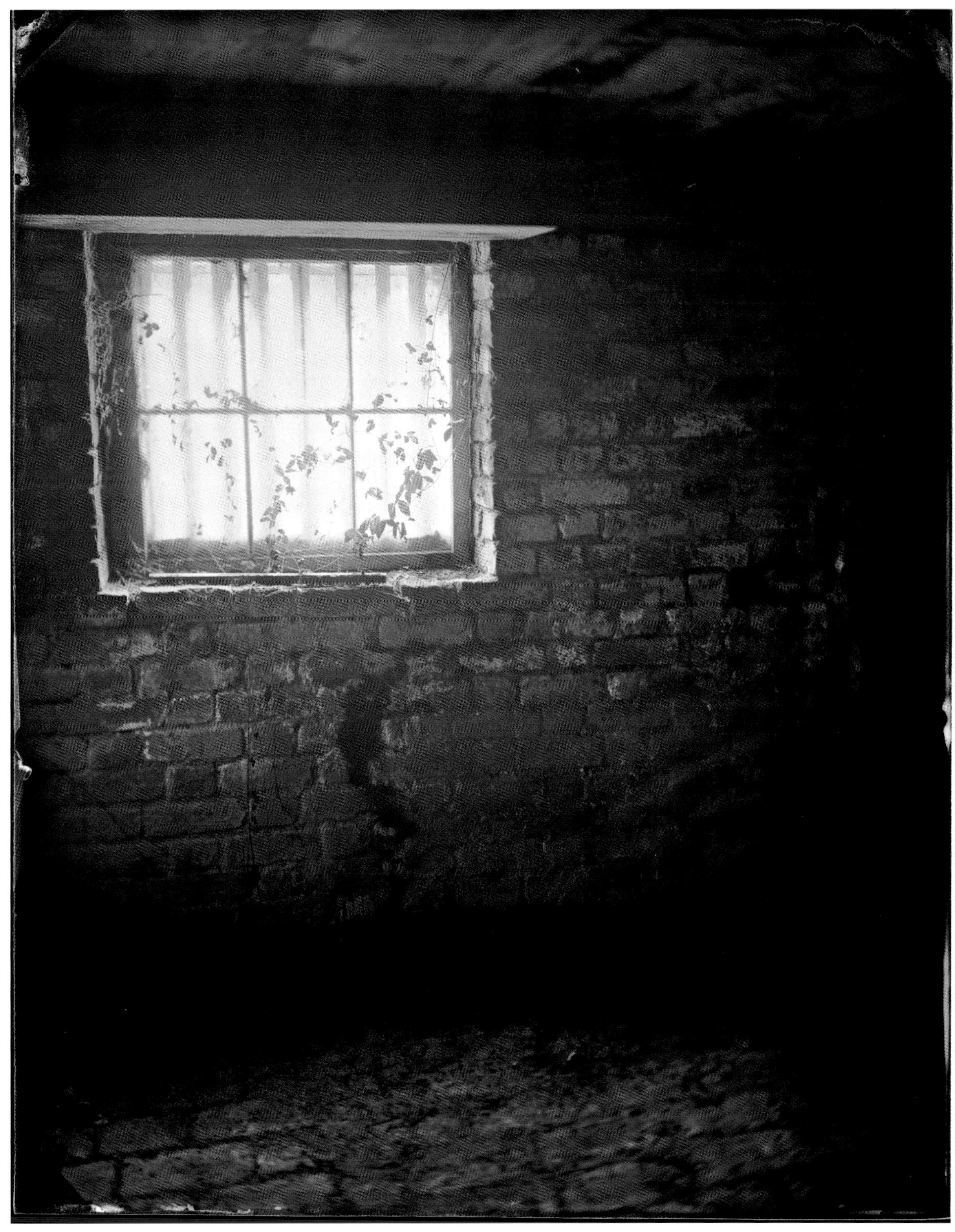

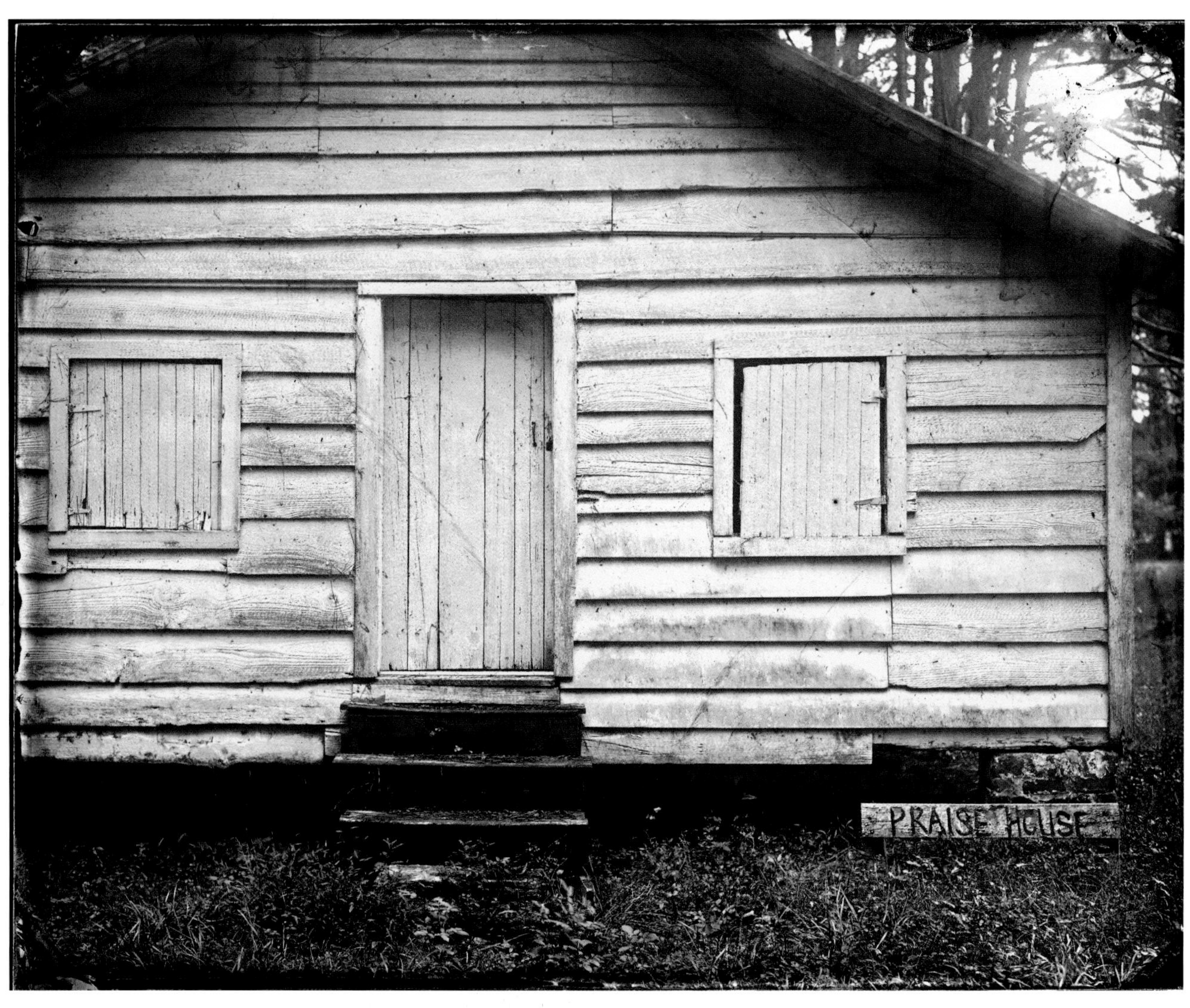

PRAISE HOUSE, YEMASSEE, SOUTH CAROLINA
Enslaved people celebrated a mix of African and Christian faith traditions in these wooden structures. This praise house overlooks the Combahee River on the Inner Passage route.

DOCKS ON BOHICKET CREEK
In the 1700s and 1800s, this estuary where Bohicket Creek and the North Edisto River converge was one of the most dangerous sections of the Inner Passage because the open water exposed travelers to high winds and sea storms.

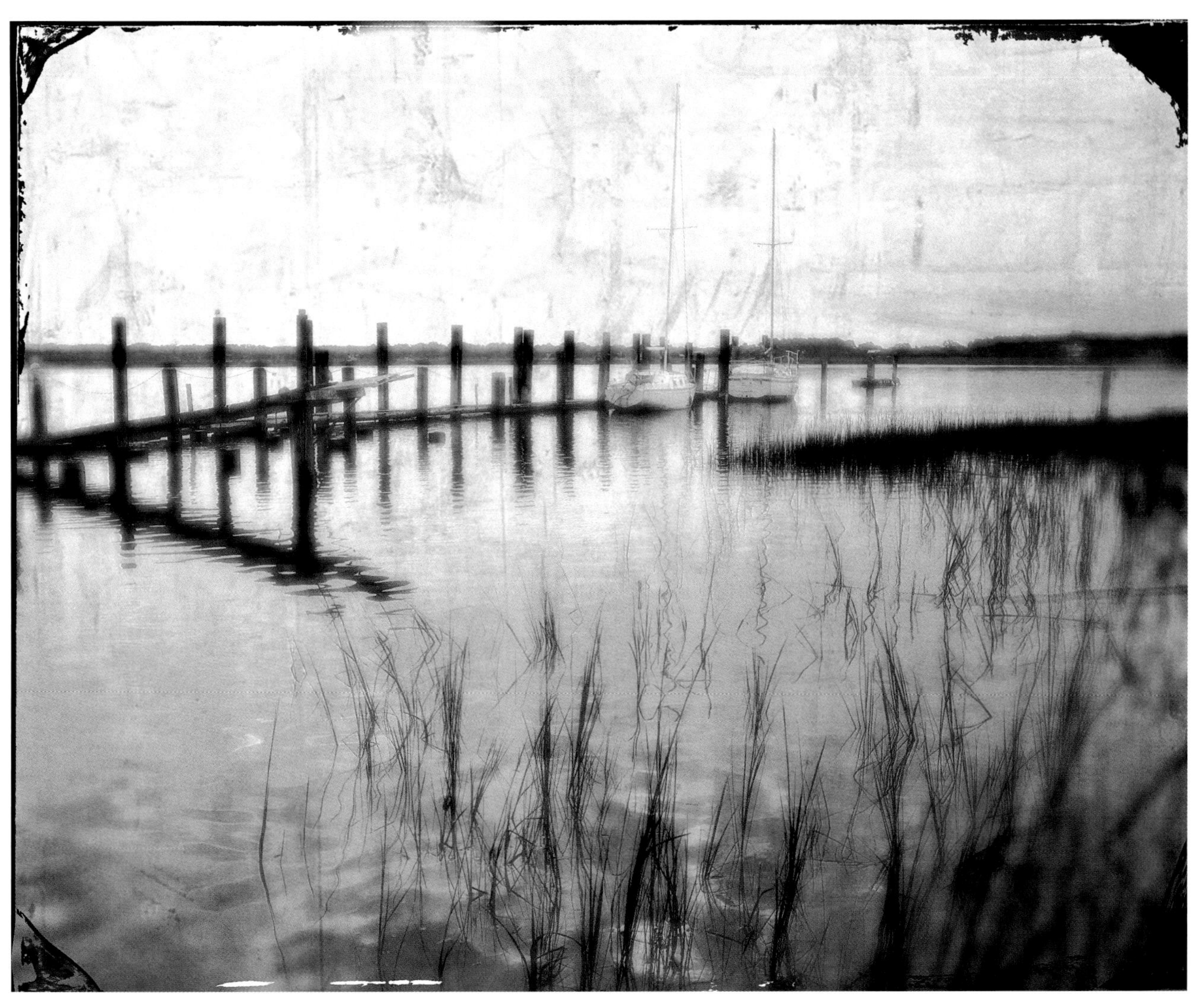

EVENING FIELDS ALONG BOHICKET CREEK
Agricultural fields on Wadmalaw Island have been farmed for centuries.

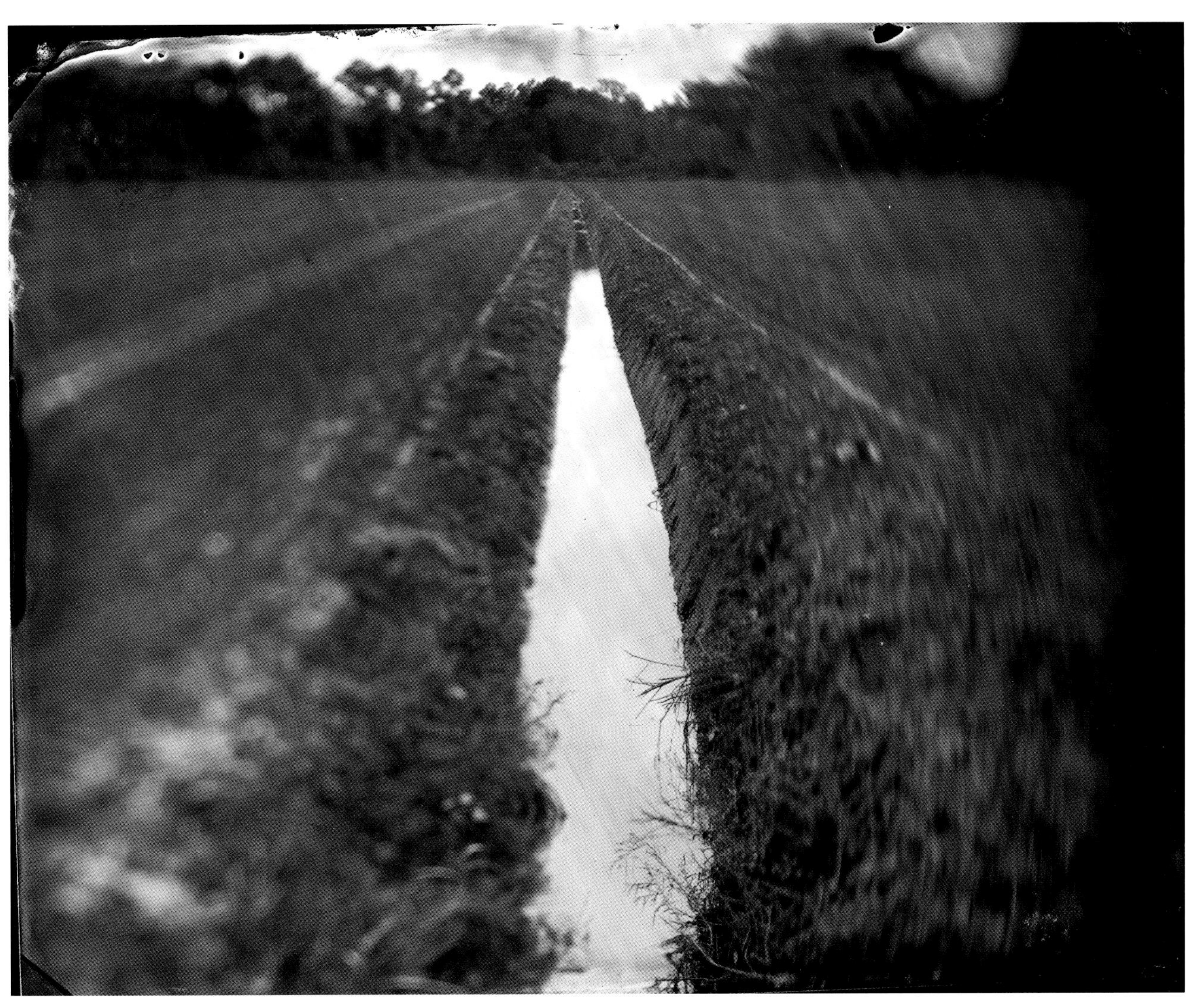

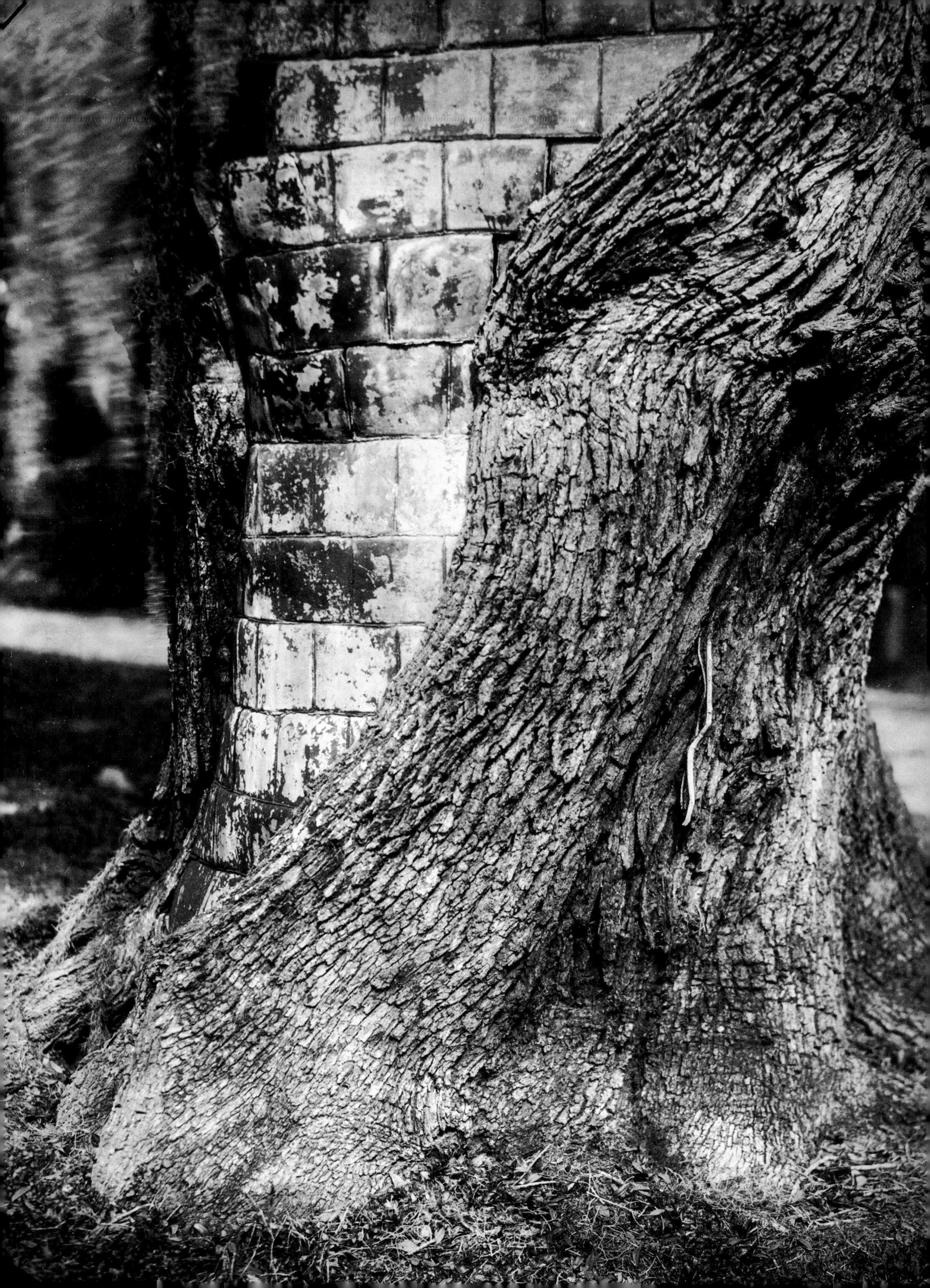

LIVE OAK WITH CINDER BLOCKS, COLLETON COUNTY
Concrete and cinder blocks stabilize an ancient tree that stands in an oak allee on a plantation road leading to the Inner Passage.

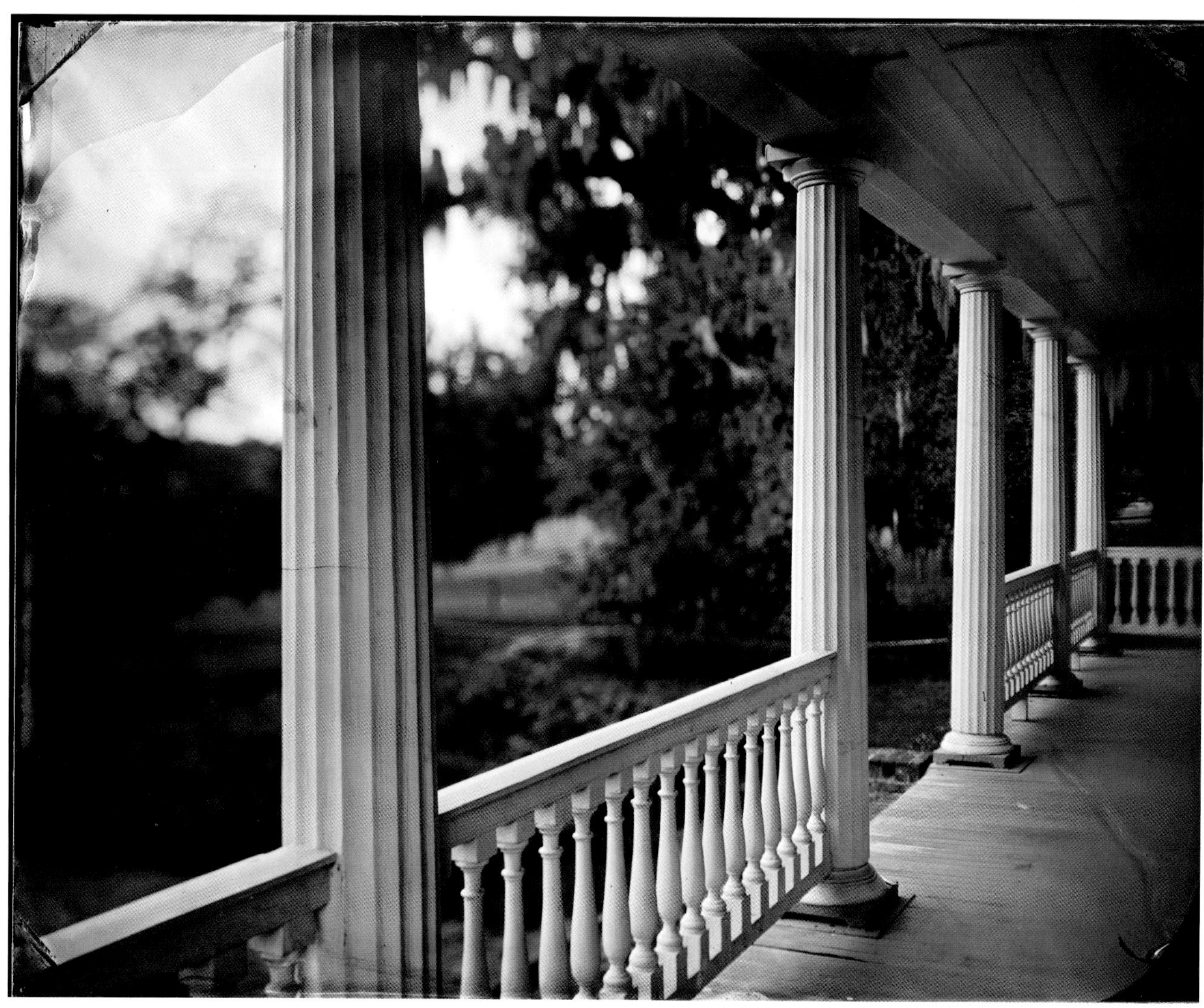

VIEW FROM THE PORCH, MCLEOD PLANTATION, JAMES ISLAND
A plantation house porch overlooks former cotton fields beside Wappoo Cut.

NEW CUT ROAD, WADMALAW ISLAND
For over two hundred years, people living on Wadmalaw Island used this sandy road to reach the New Cut boat landing where a ferry collected travelers and carried them twenty-five miles to Charleston. Although the ferry service was discontinued in the 1900s, the roadbed remains.

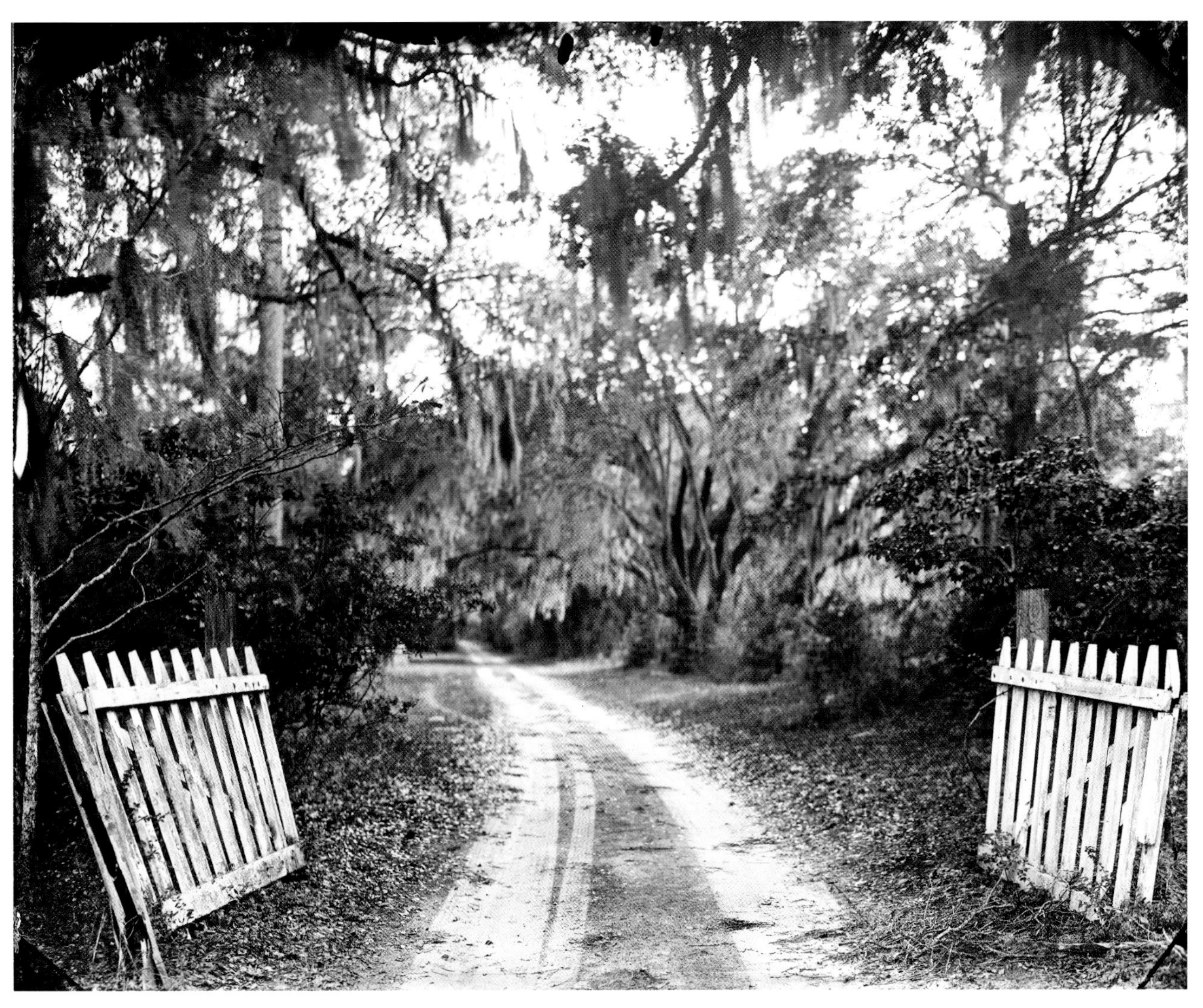

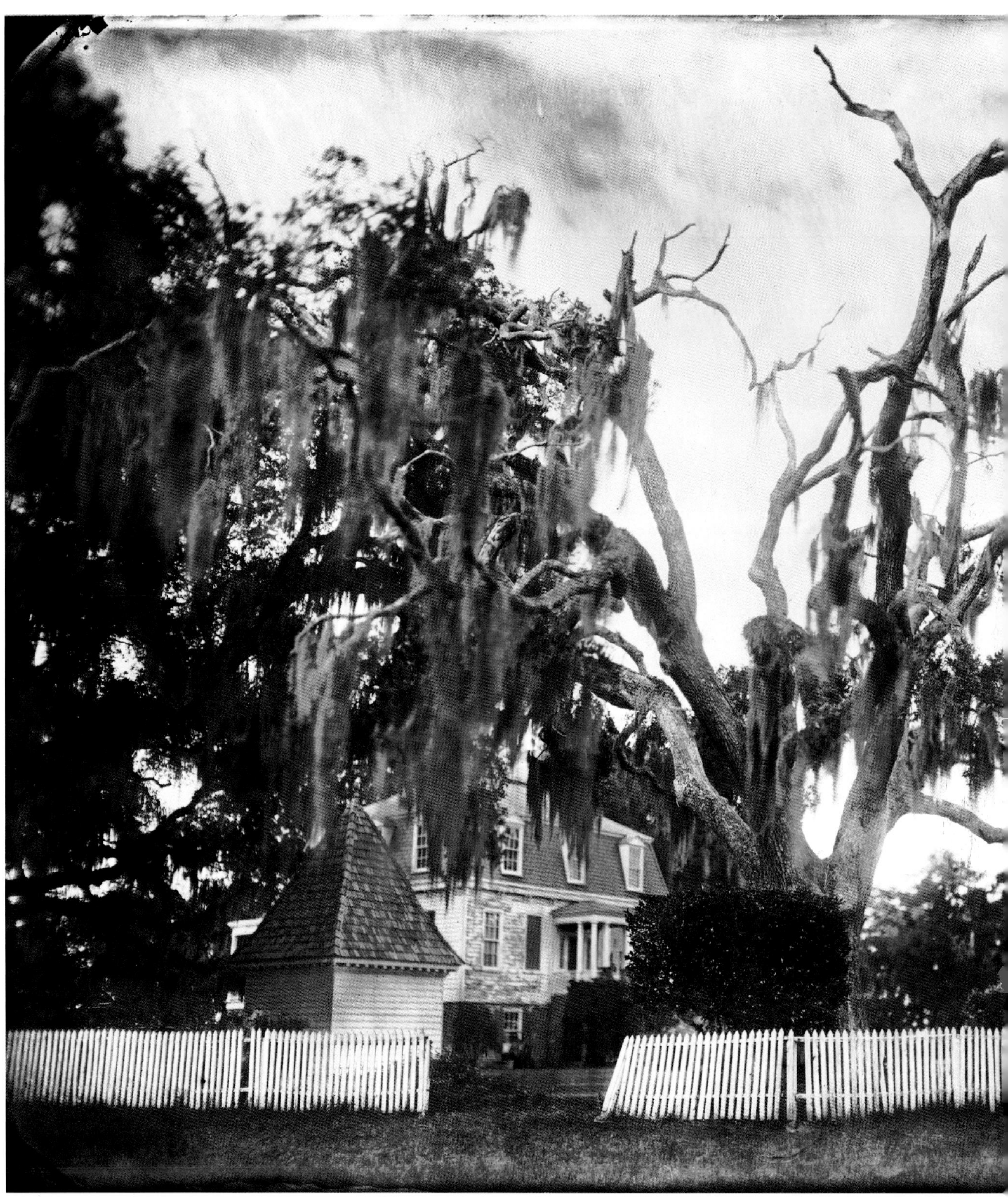

NEW CUT, WADMALAW ISLAND
New Cut suffered damage from Hurricane Ian in 2022. In the 1700s and 1800s, enslaved men between the ages of sixteen and sixty were forced to clear hurricane debris from the Inner Passage.

PON PON CHAPEL, NEAR THE STONO RIVER IN COLLETON COUNTY

A ruin known as the Burnt Church was originally built for colonial parishioners in the 1700s. The church facade shown in this photograph is no longer standing.

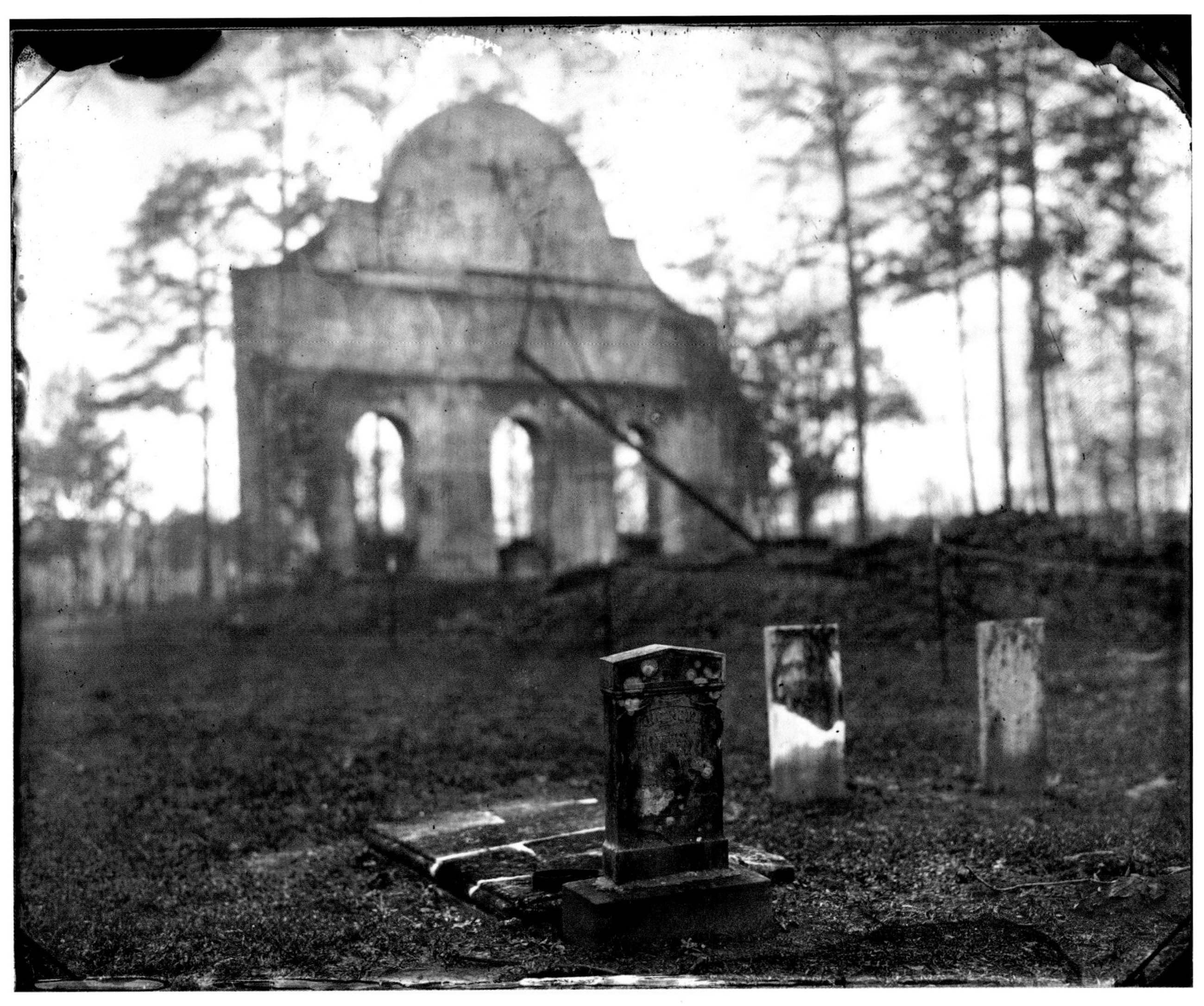

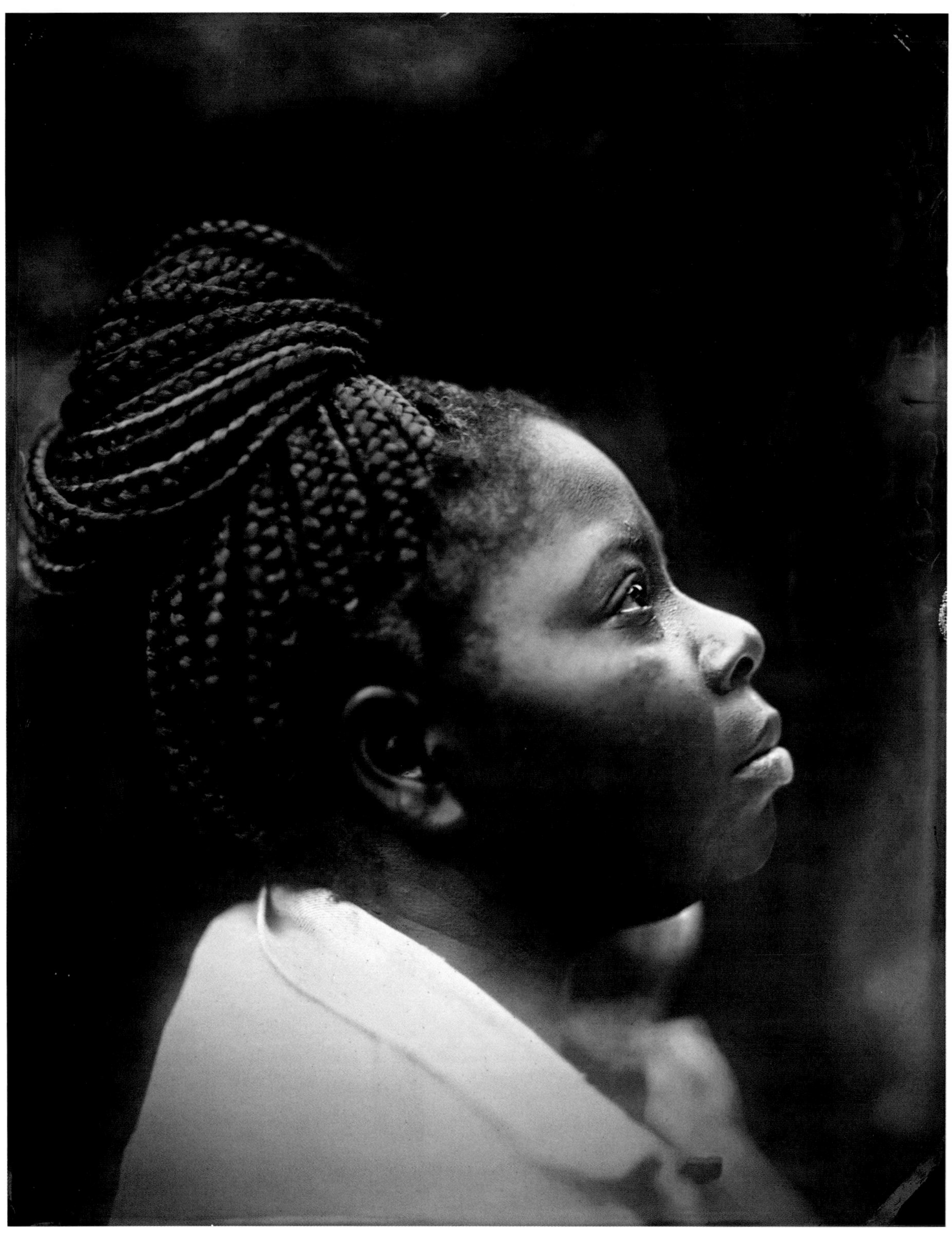

NICOLE MOORE, NATIVE OF CHARLESTON

Nicole Moore's family has lived for generations in Charleston, with strong familial ties to Edisto, Johns, and James Islands. She takes pride in her many Lowcountry ancestors, including Mary Mathews Just, a teacher and community activist who led the effort to start an African American community after the Civil War. In 1886, several Black families purchased farmland from a former plantation and called their new town "Maryville" in honor of Moore's relative.

IRVIN MCKNIGHT, RAVENEL
Irvin McKnight is a commercial waterman who fishes on the rivers and estuaries of the Inner Passage.

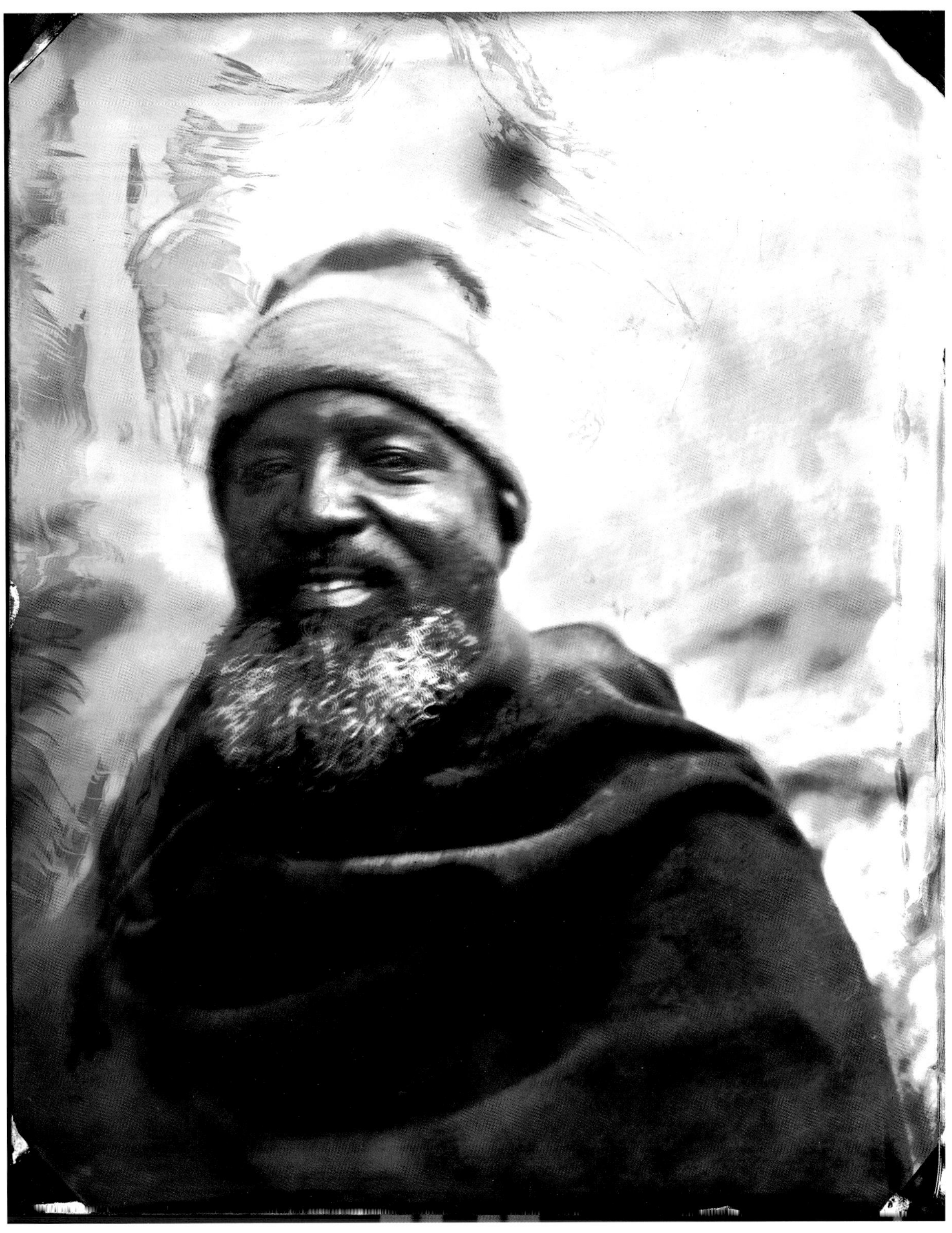

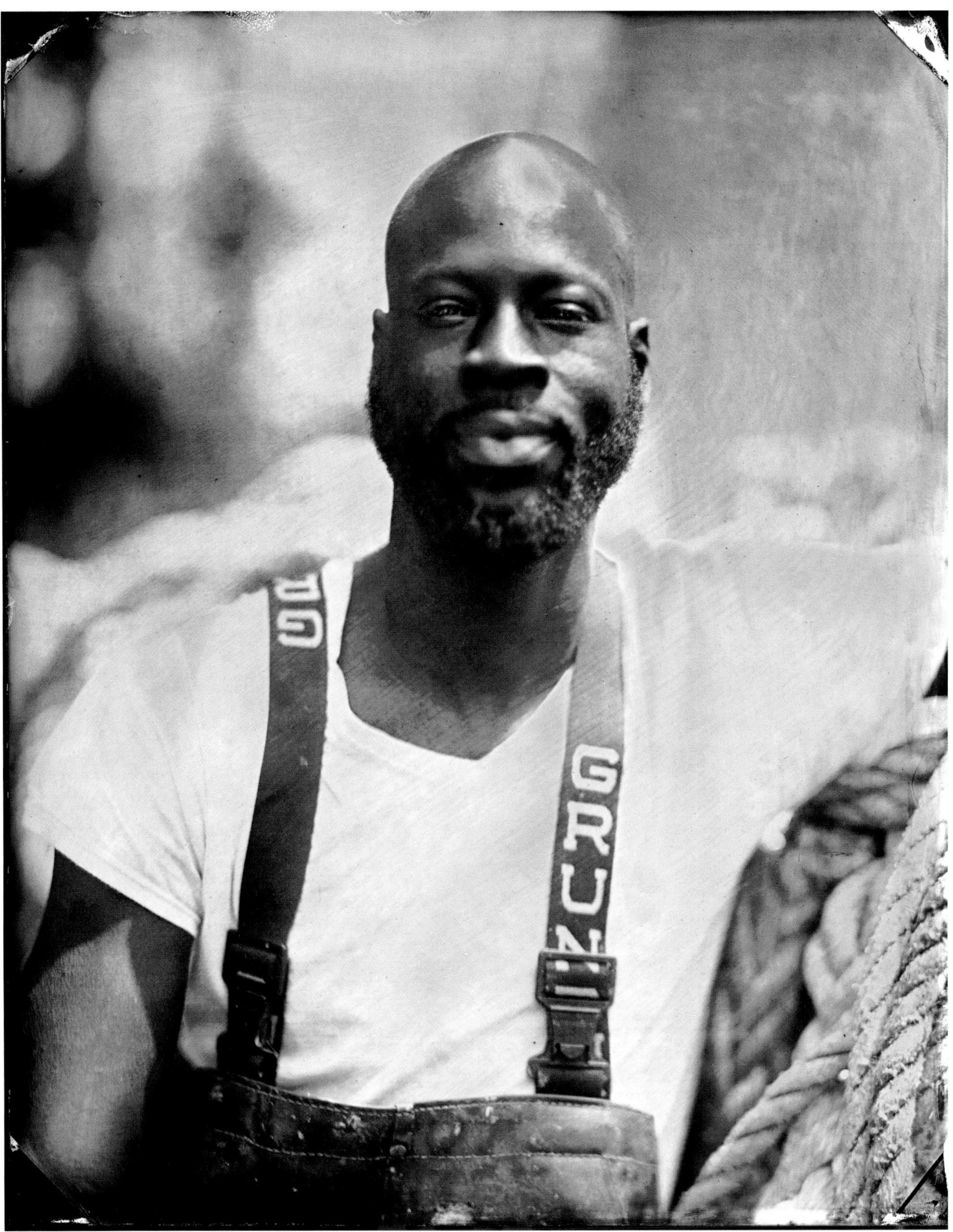

I was raised on Roosevelt Road off Cherry Point Road here on Wadmalaw Island. All of my grandparents—from my mother's family and my father's family—were from the islands. My grandparents met out here as children and they were raised together. My grandfathers were both half Cherokee. My great-grandmother, she died when she was 113. Her house is the first white house on the left around the bend from the docks here on Wadmalaw. She was full-blooded African. And my dad's grandfather was full-blooded African. If you go past the barbeque place on the road leaving Wadmalaw Island, there's a little graveyard and I have relatives in there. Native American family relatives buried right there. Washingtons.

SHERMAN MACK, WADMALAW ISLAND
Sherman Mack is an artist and waterman whose family has lived by the Inner Passage for over 150 years.

DANIEL STEVENS LAROCHE, WADMALAW ISLAND
The LaRoches trace their ancestry on Wadmalaw Island back to the early 1800s. Captain Robert Sandford landed on Wadmalaw Island in 1666 and, using a ceremony known as "turf and twig," claimed it as English soil.

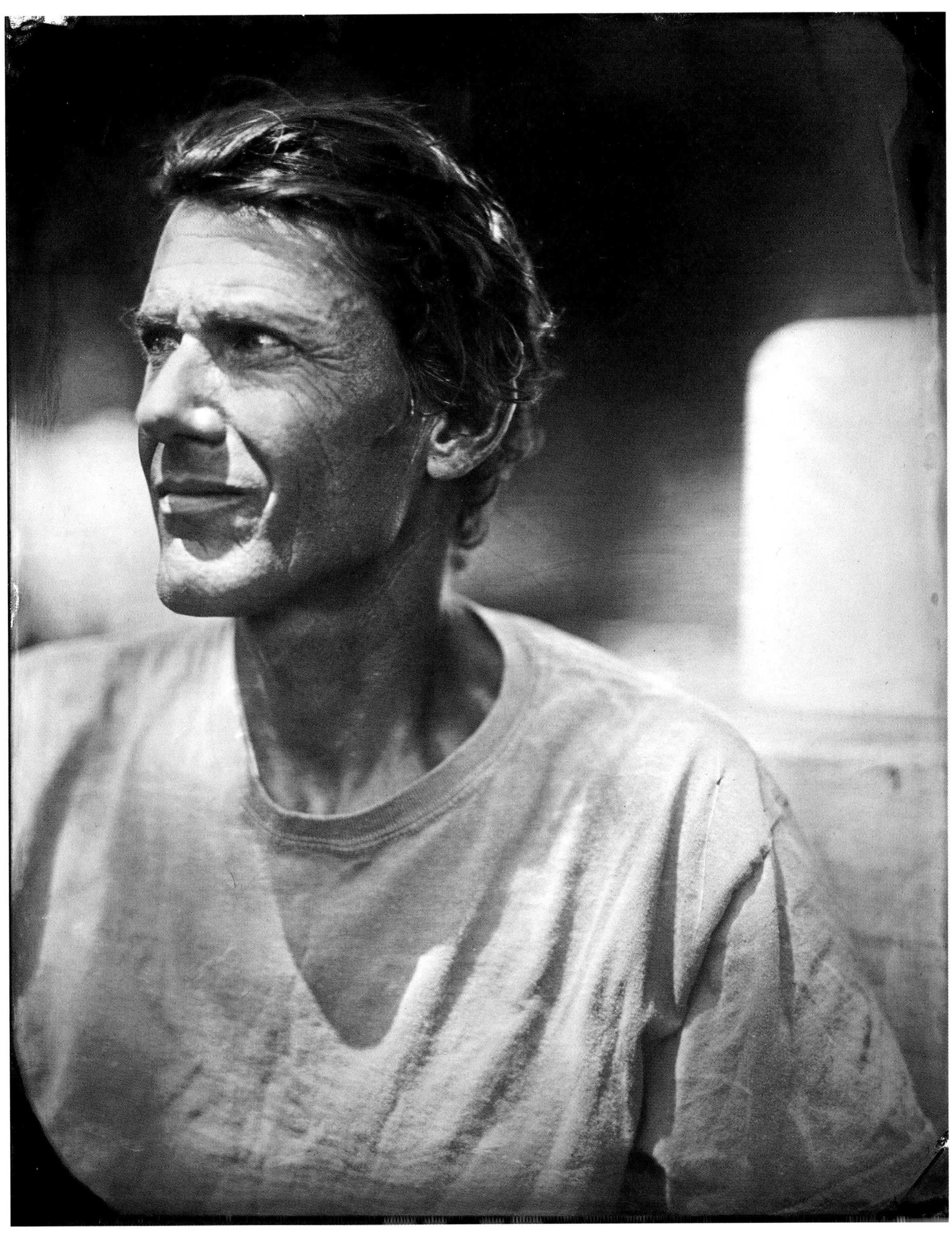

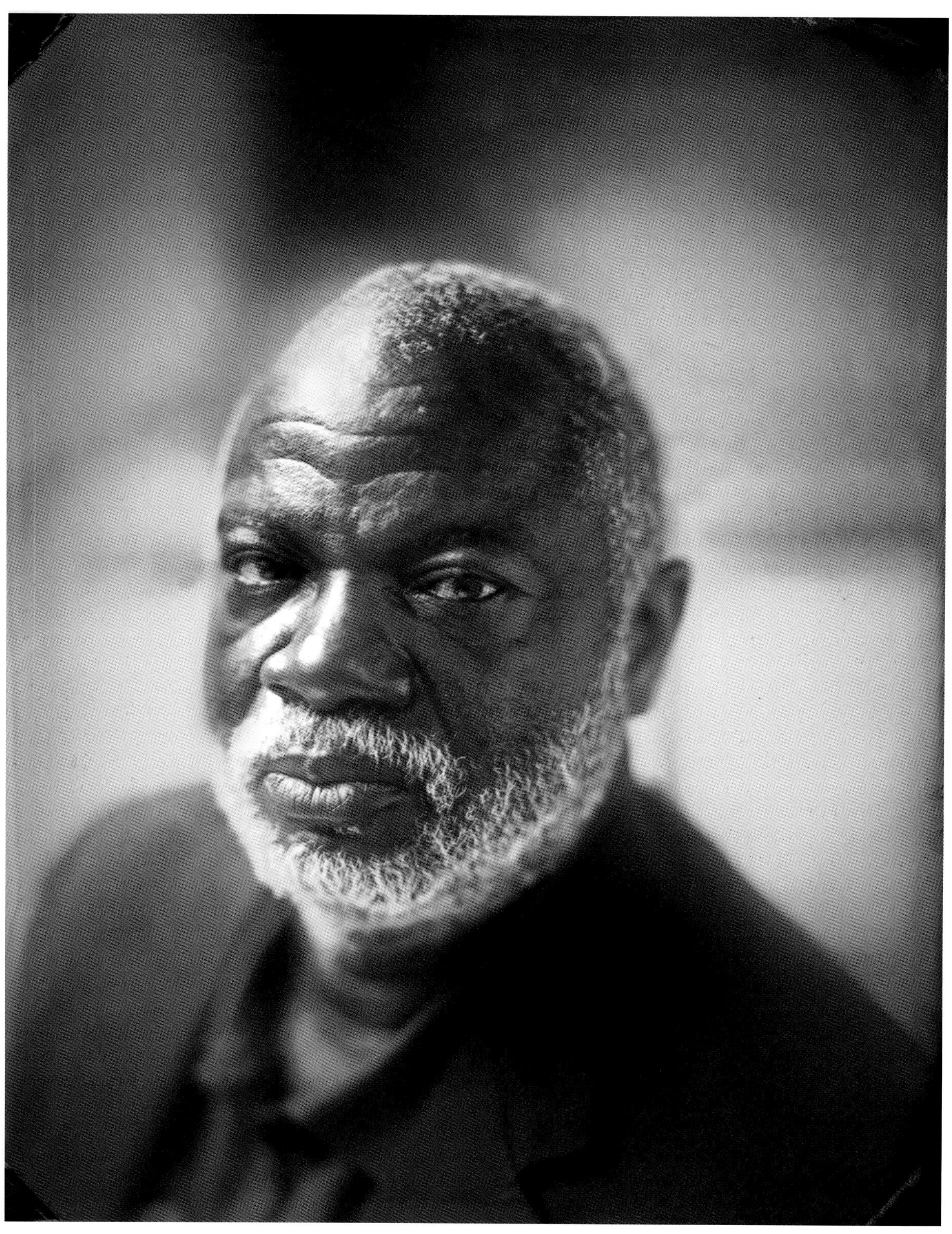

So I decided to begin sleeping in slave dwellings to become intimate with the spaces where they slept.

I was educated in South Carolina, where our teachers taught us that our ancestors were happy to be enslaved and that white enslavers were good to them. Those were all lies. I had to rid myself of those thoughts and do the research necessary to discover that I come from a proud past. Having that knowledge gave me the desire to redeem my ancestors, give them the respect they deserve, and connect with the truth of their lives. So I decided to begin sleeping in slave dwellings to become intimate with the spaces where they slept. People who lived in those slave dwellings were not a footnote in American history.

JOSEPH MCGILL, LADSON, SOUTH CAROLINA
Joseph McGill, author and the founder of the Slave Dwelling Project, has slept in over a hundred slave dwellings to honor his ancestors. Many of the places where he has slept, including McLeod Plantation, Osabaw Island, Daufuskie Island, and the BB Sams House, are located along the Inner Passage.

During slavery, they had no voice.

I am a Charlestonian. I grew up on the east side of Charleston on the peninsula, where I attended Mother Emanuel Church. Over the past decades I've worked as a journalist, author, and historian in South Carolina. Place is a powerful thing. In my writing, I am trying to bring forward the ancestors' experiences, the good times and the bad times, to give them a voice. During slavery, they had no voice.

HERB FRAZIER, SUMMERVILLE, SOUTH CAROLINA
Herb Frazier, an author of books about Black culture in South Carolina, kayaks through Lowcountry rivers as homage to his African ancestors' water culture.

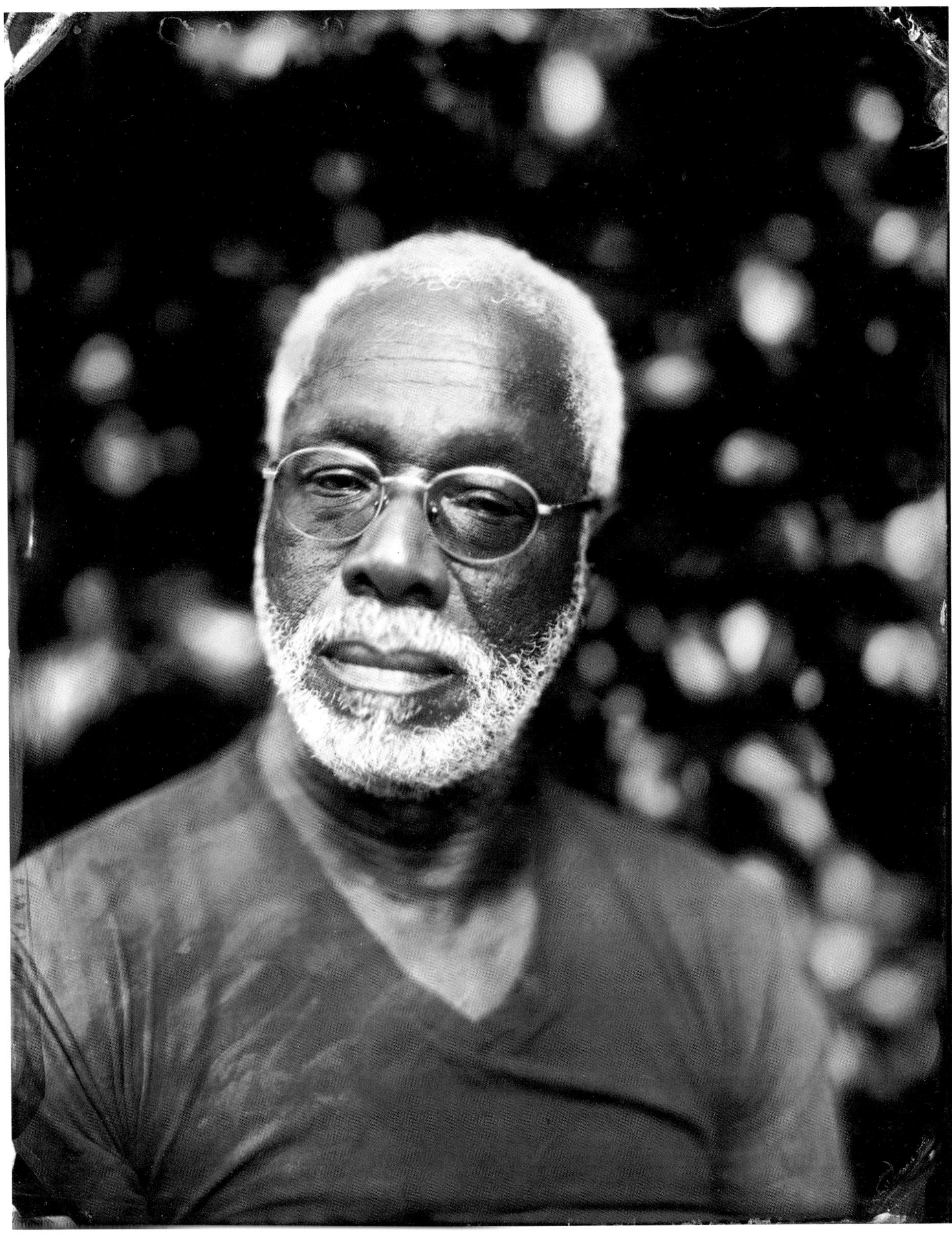

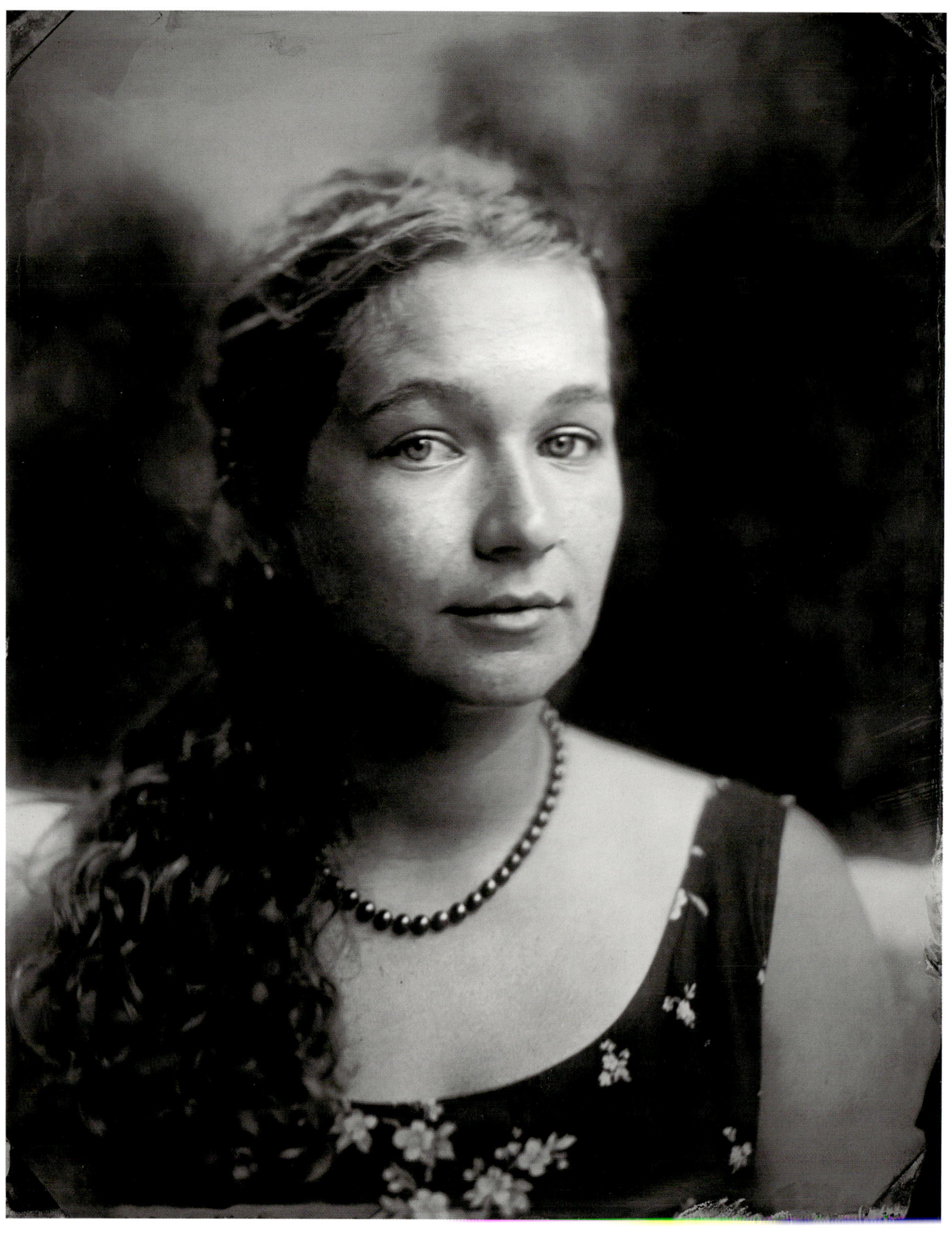

The barrier between past and present is thin in certain parts of South Carolina.

The barrier between past and present is thin in certain parts of South Carolina. Hearing my family speak in Lowcountry dialect helps me travel back in time. The Lowcountry accent is so familiar. My great-grandmother, Gigi, is still alive. She's ninety-two and lives in South Carolina. A lot of my childhood memories of South Carolina come from my travels to Gigi's house. Watching the trees go by through the car window. Watching the swamp go by. I became interested in South Carolina history because of Grandma Gigi's stories about ghosts. My Grandmother Gigi still talks about boo daddies, hags, and haints. The stories Gigi would tell made me afraid of looking out the window into the swamp at night.

CHEYENNE KOTH LEAHY, ST. AUGUSTINE, FLORIDA
Cheyenne Koth Leahy is a Charleston native whose family arrived in the Lowcountry before the Civil War. Koth Leahy works as a cultural historian studying the histories of Black people who escaped slavery in Carolina and found freedom in St. Augustine in the 1700s.

He would tell me about slavery.

My family, the Mitchells, were first in Charleston and then they came out of South Carolina, moving north after slavery ended. I remember sitting on my grandfather Asbury Mitchell's lap when I was a boy in the 1950s. He would tell me about slavery. He was an old guy—about eighty or ninety years old. Listening to his stories of survival inspired me to join the Fort Mose Militia in St. Augustine, Florida. Each year the militia dresses up in colonial-era military uniforms to honor the hundreds of Black soldiers who protected Fort Mose, the first free Black community in America.

LLOYD MITCHELL, ST. AUGUSTINE, FLORIDA
Lloyd Mitchell's family lived in South Carolina before the Civil War.

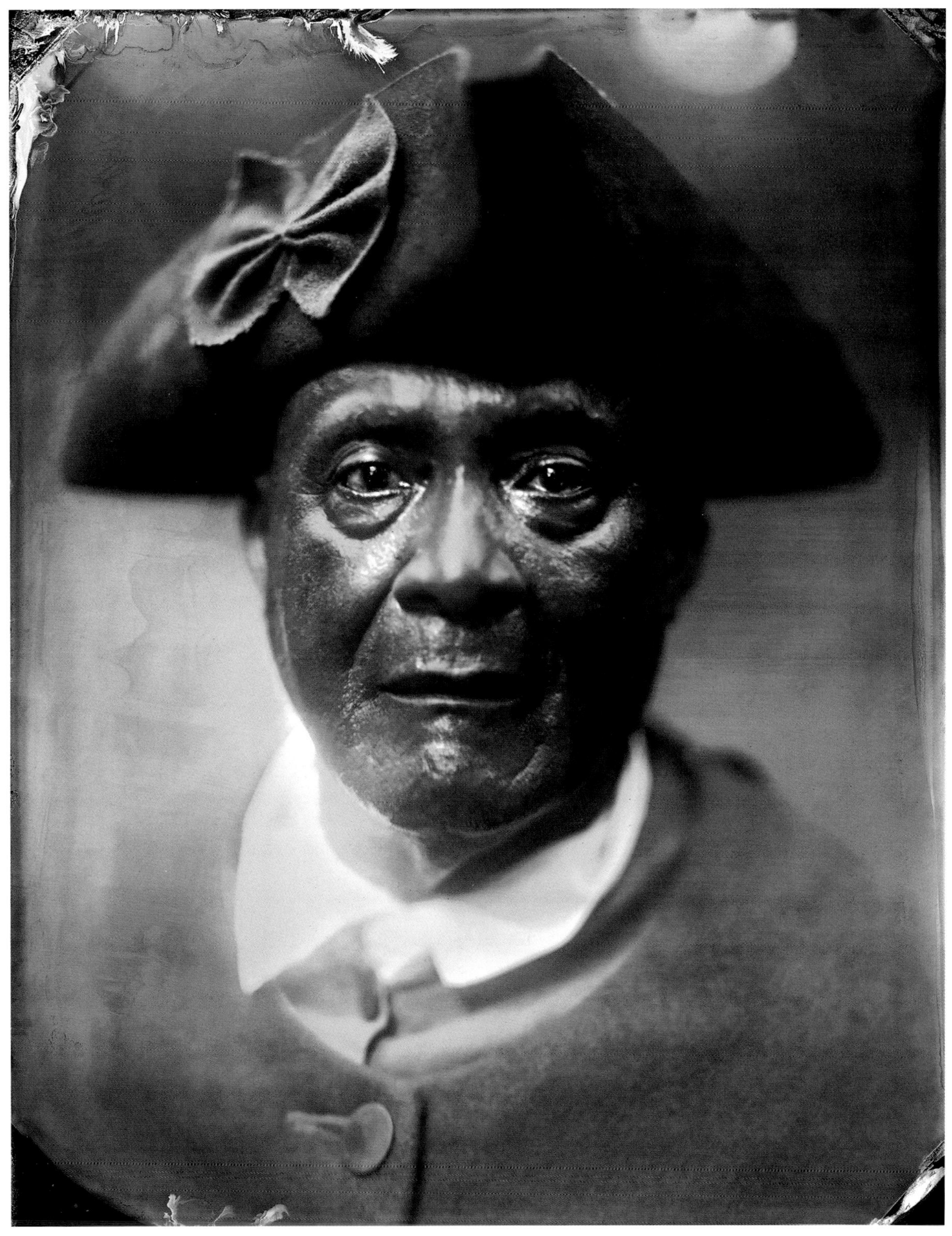

I sat on porches and listened to the oral stories from my kin.

When I was growing up, we got in the car twice a year and drove to my grandparents' house in Charleston. Mostly we just sat on the porch with the admonition that "children should be seen and not heard." I was expected to just sit and listen to my elders. I would hear stories about the family, the community, the catching up. And then there were those older stories about the family history. My dad's side of the family. Slavery. Civil War. Sharecroppers. Civil rights. Those were the porch stories that I heard about all my life. I hear and understand the history of the Civil War differently because I sat on porches and listened to the oral stories from my kin.

HILARY GREEN, CAROLINA
Hilary Green learned her family's history by sitting on the porches of her Charleston relatives.

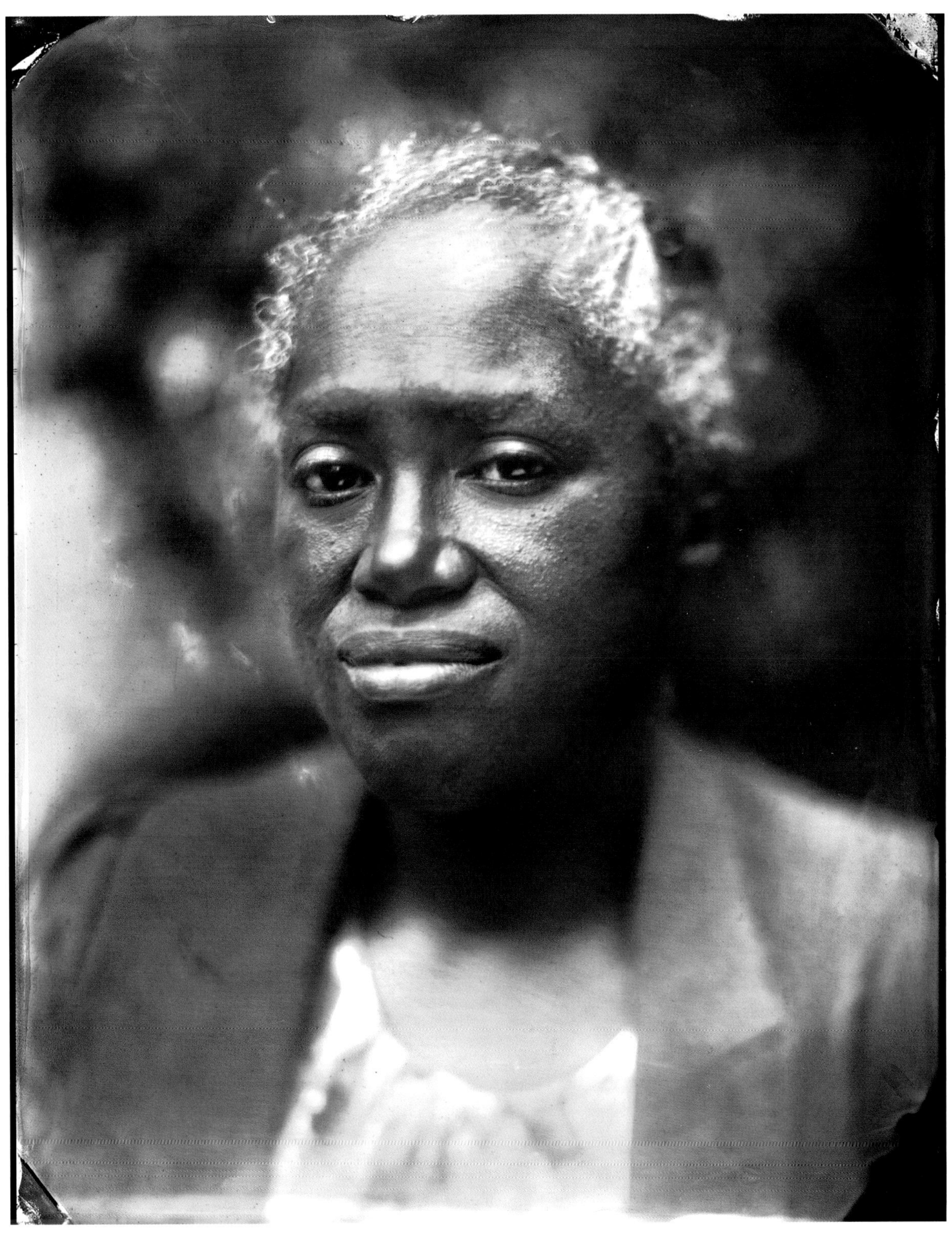

AERIAL VIEW SOUTHWARD OVER THE STONO RIVER, CHARLESTON

In the 1700s and 1800s, settlers and merchants living on the Sea Islands south of Charleston traveled by boat on the Stono River to reach Charleston.

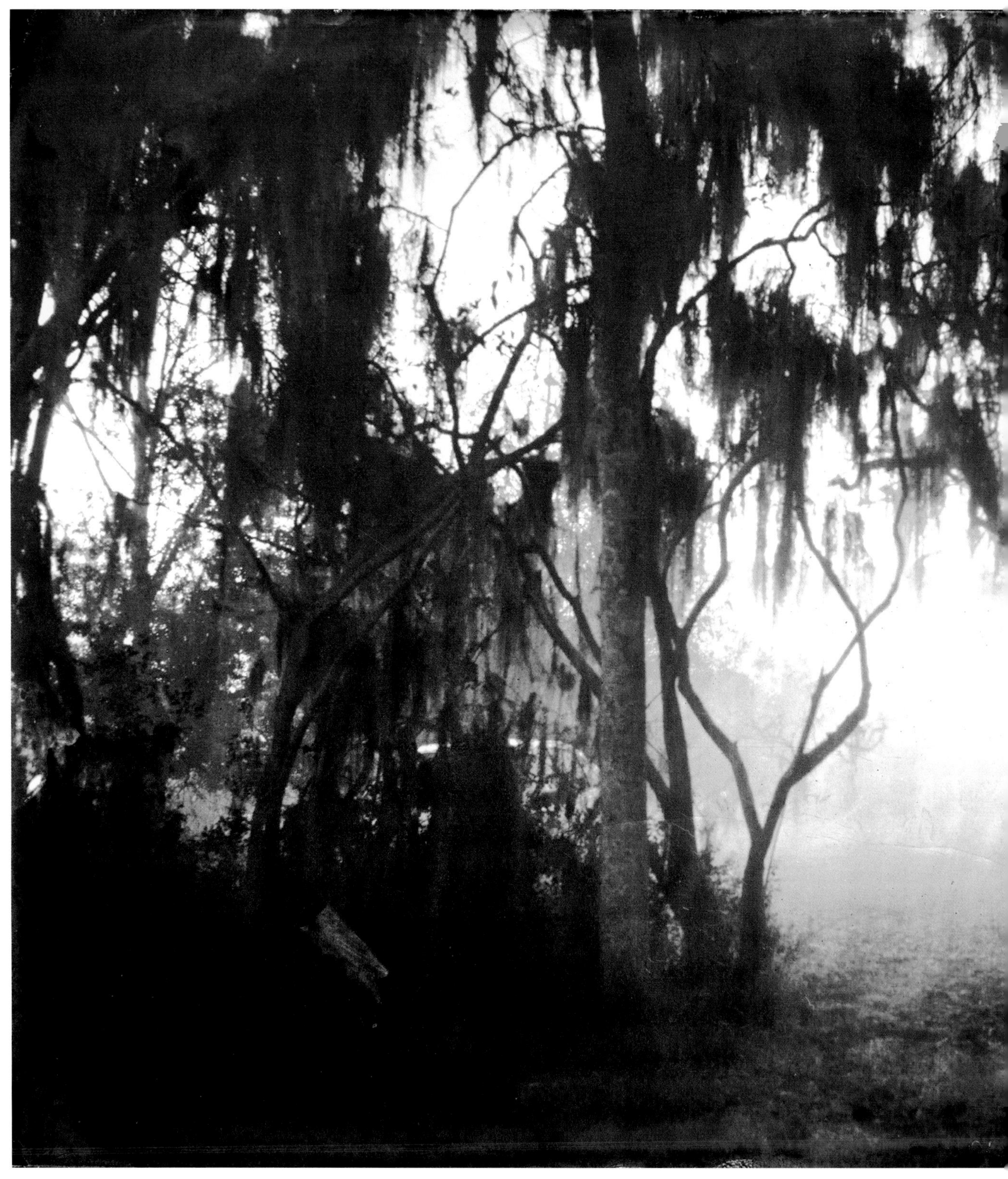

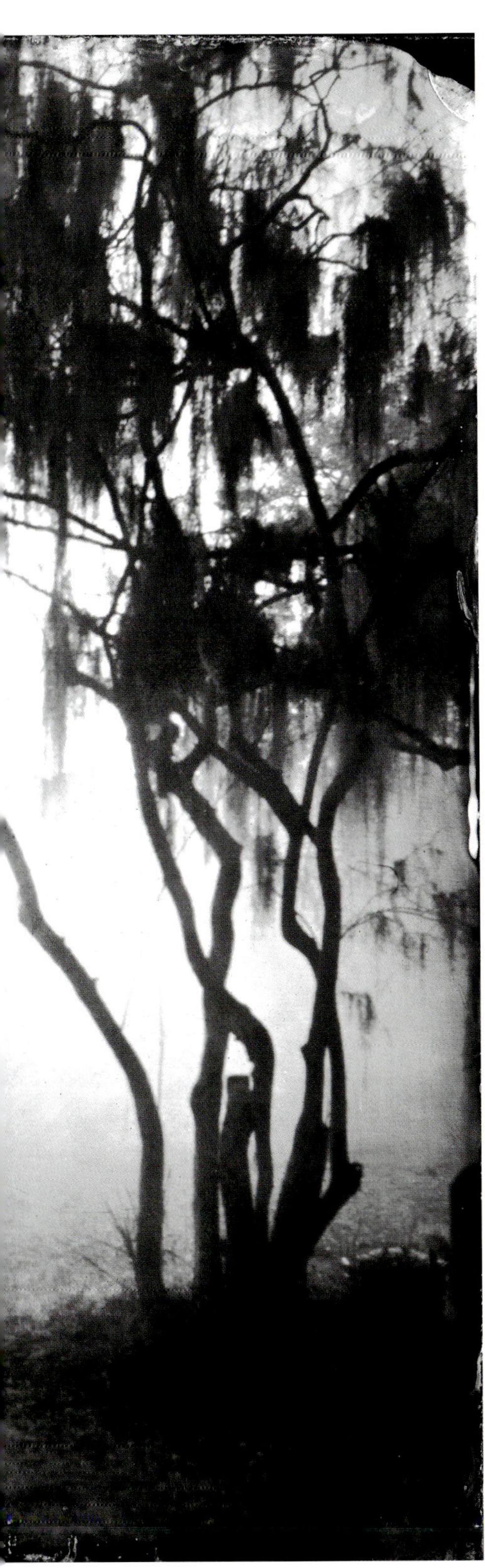

MORNING AT NEW CUT
Spanish moss, a native perennial herb, covers trees around a footpath leading to New Cut. Spanish moss grows on the branches of live oaks and pines in the semitropical Lowcountry of South Carolina.

TWILIGHT AT NEW CUT
In the 1700s and 1800s, enslaved people paddled canoes on the Inner Passage to escape from Carolina. The Rev. L. R. Ferebee, a formerly enslaved waterman from Carolina, remarked, "even at night I could steer by the compass, or by any star."

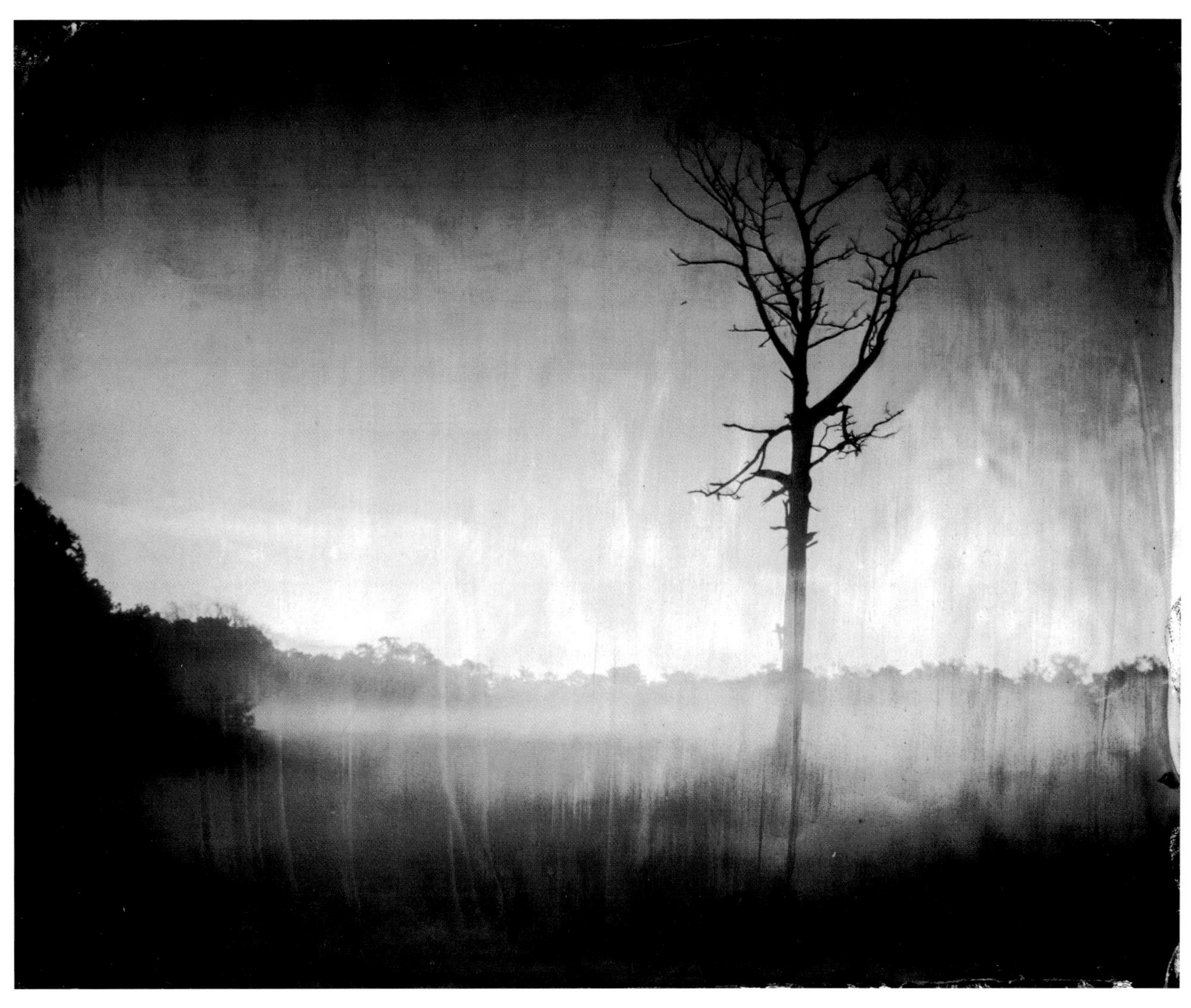

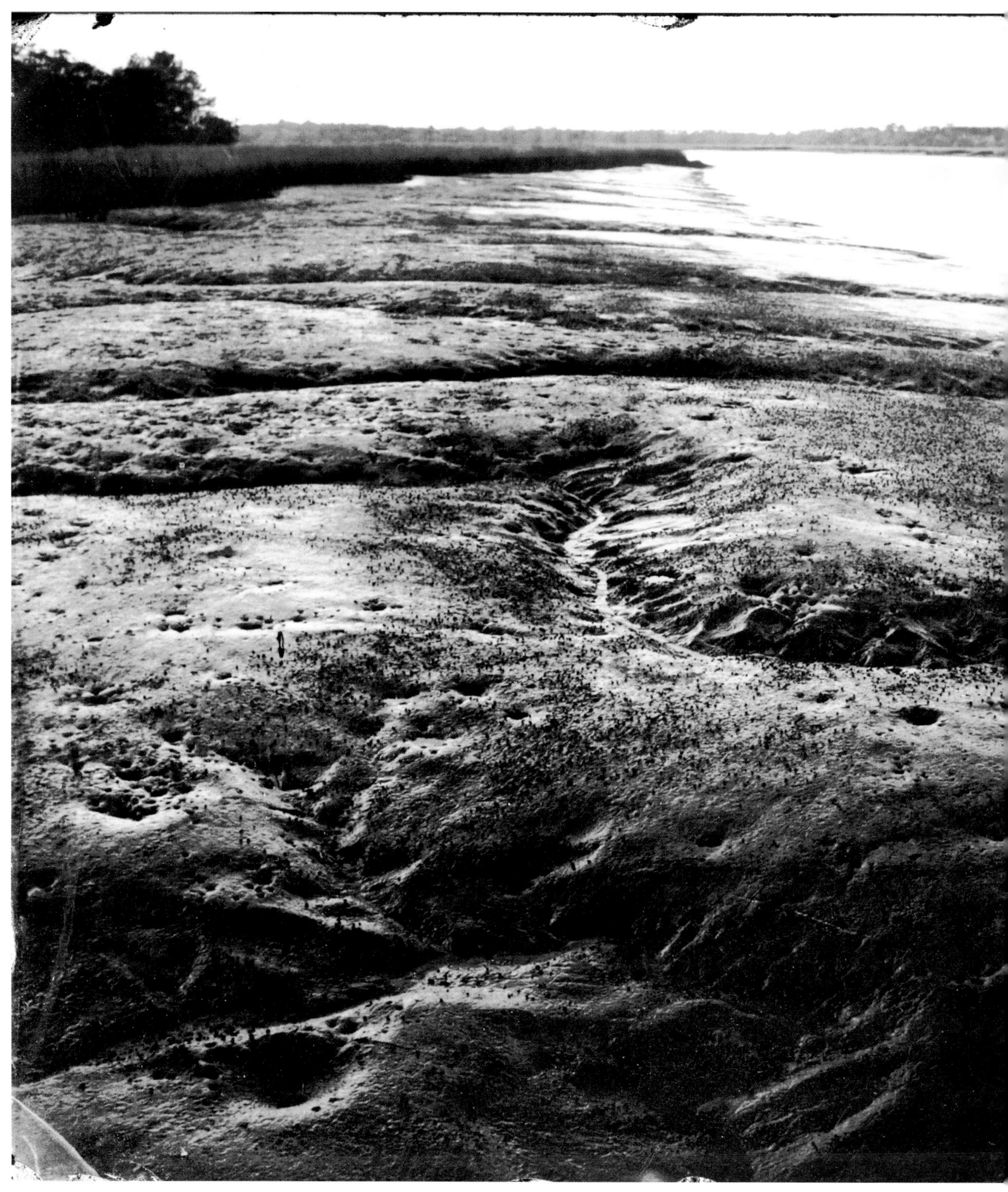

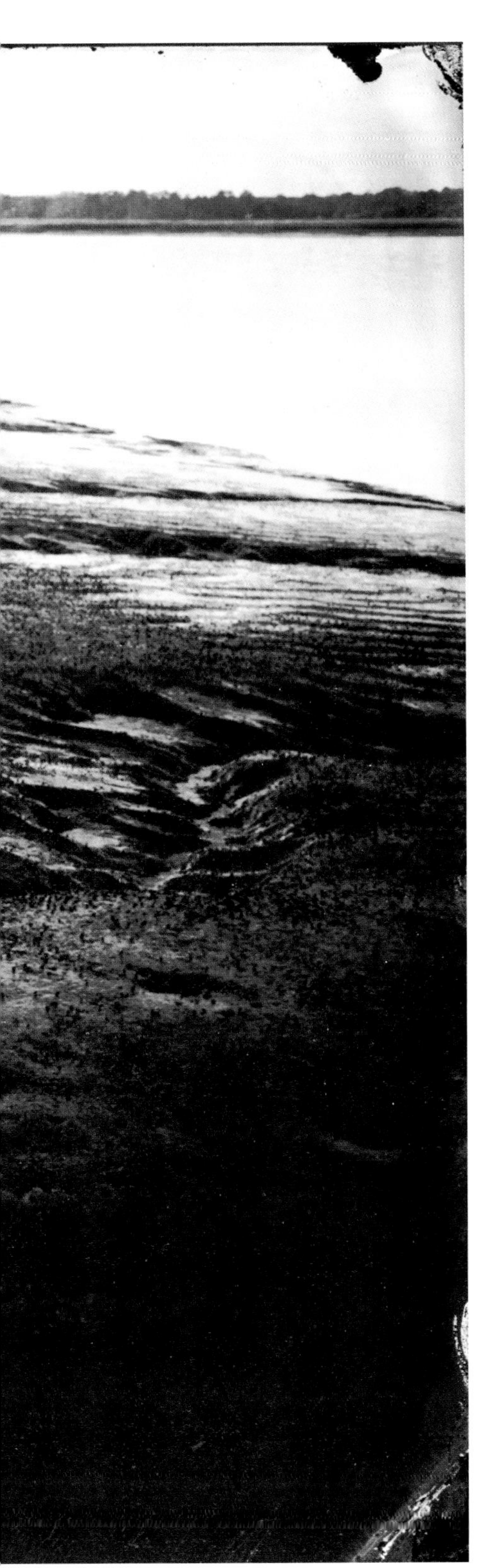

LOW TIDE, WADMALAW RIVER
Lowcountry rivers experience semidiurnal tides that regularly move over seven feet of water away from the shoreline and expose underlying pluff mud. Travelers on the Inner Passage timed their journeys with the powerful ocean tides.

WOODEN MARKER, COOPER RIVER
Grave marker for an enslaved person stands in an abandoned cemetery along the banks of the Cooper River. There is no name indicated on the marker, but seven or eight horizontal lines carved into the cedar wood have survived for over a century.

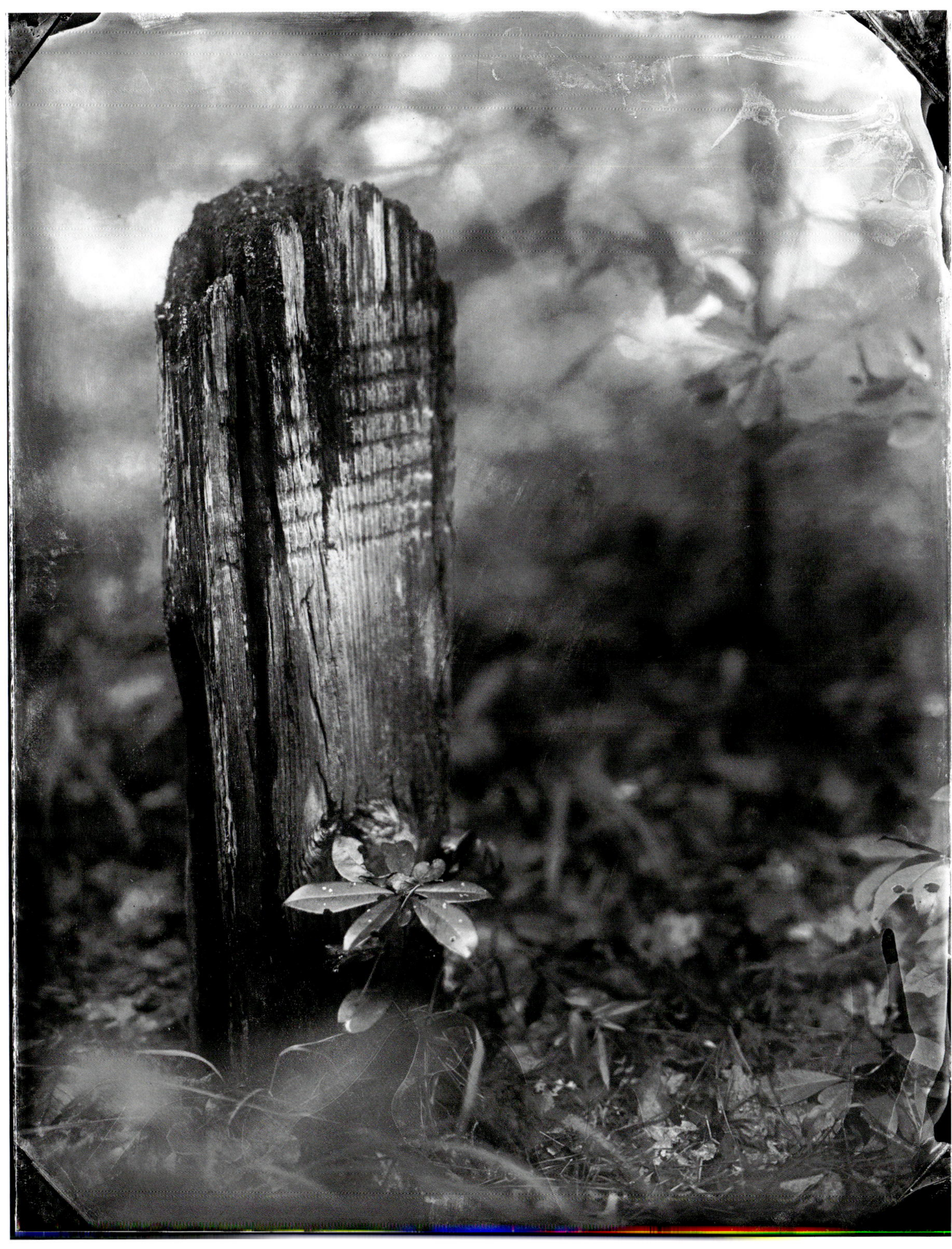

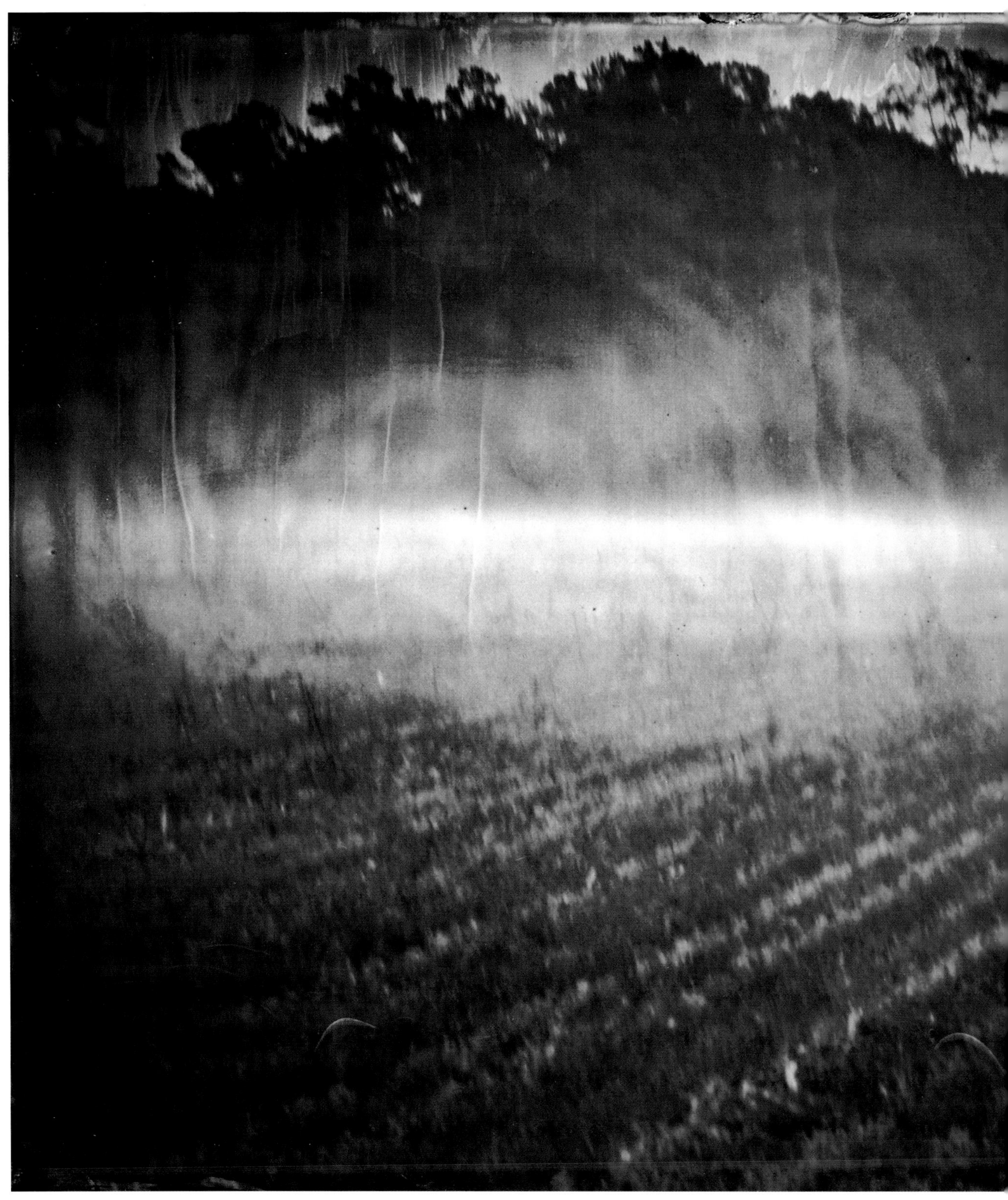

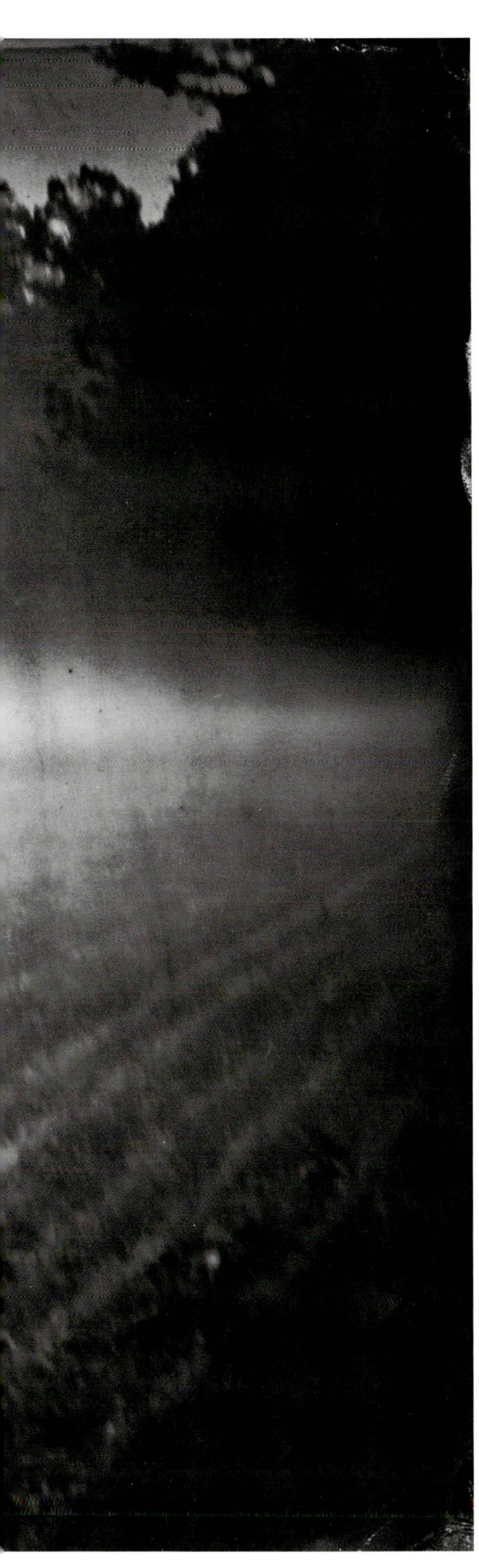

FIELD, WADMALAW ISLAND
Former agricultural field that has been farmed for over two hundred years. Planters shipped crops on the Inner Passage from Wadmalaw Island to markets in Charleston.

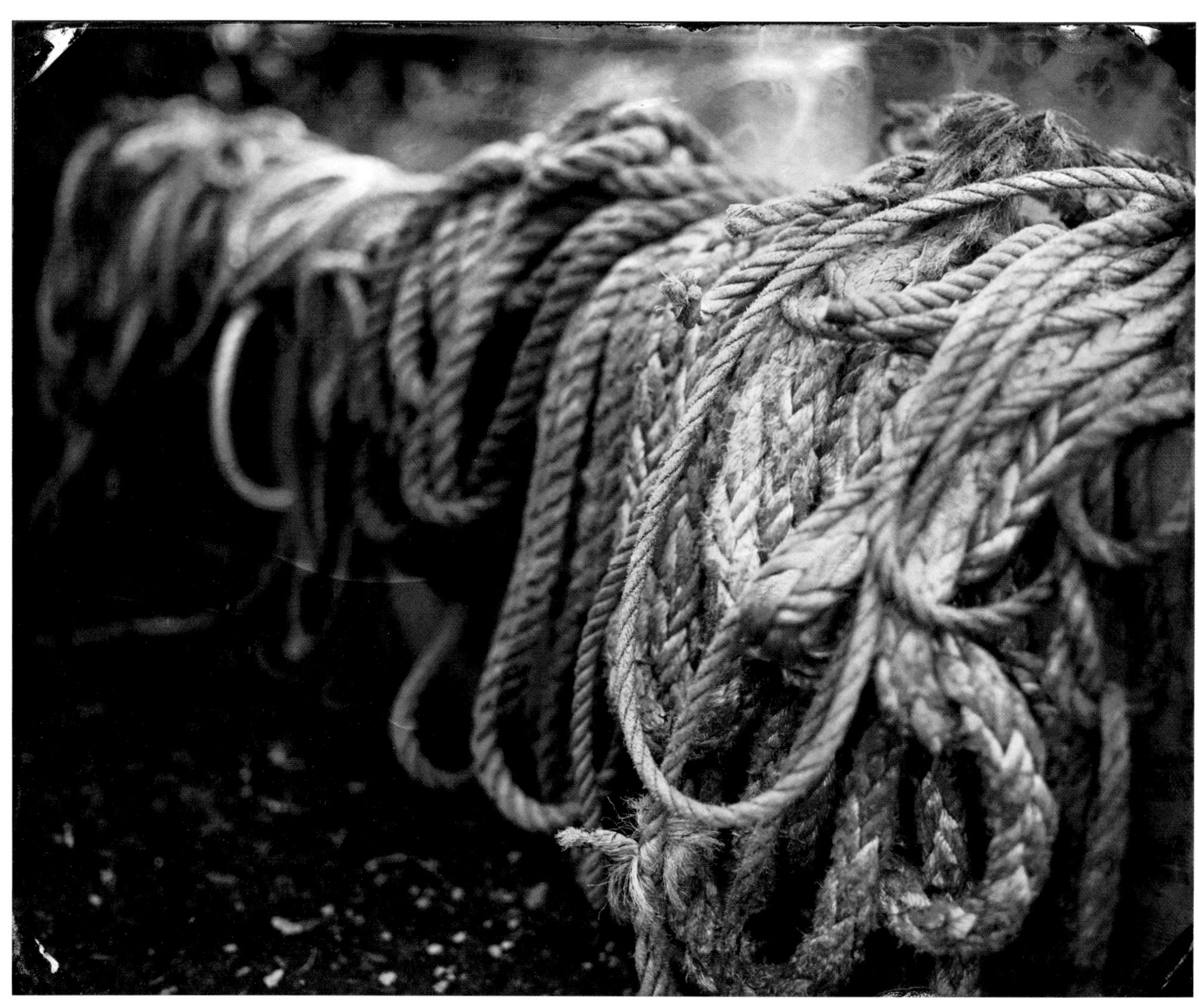

NAUTICAL ROPE, WADMALAW ISLAND
Modern-day ropes are stored outside a commercial fishery on Bohicket Creek. In the 1700s, boats traveled through Bohicket Creek and nearby Haulover Cut to reach Charleston.

WOODEN BOAT HULL
In the 1700s, enslaved men paddled this boat carrying bricks on the Inner Passage toward Charleston. On the way, the boat and its cargo sank in the Black River.

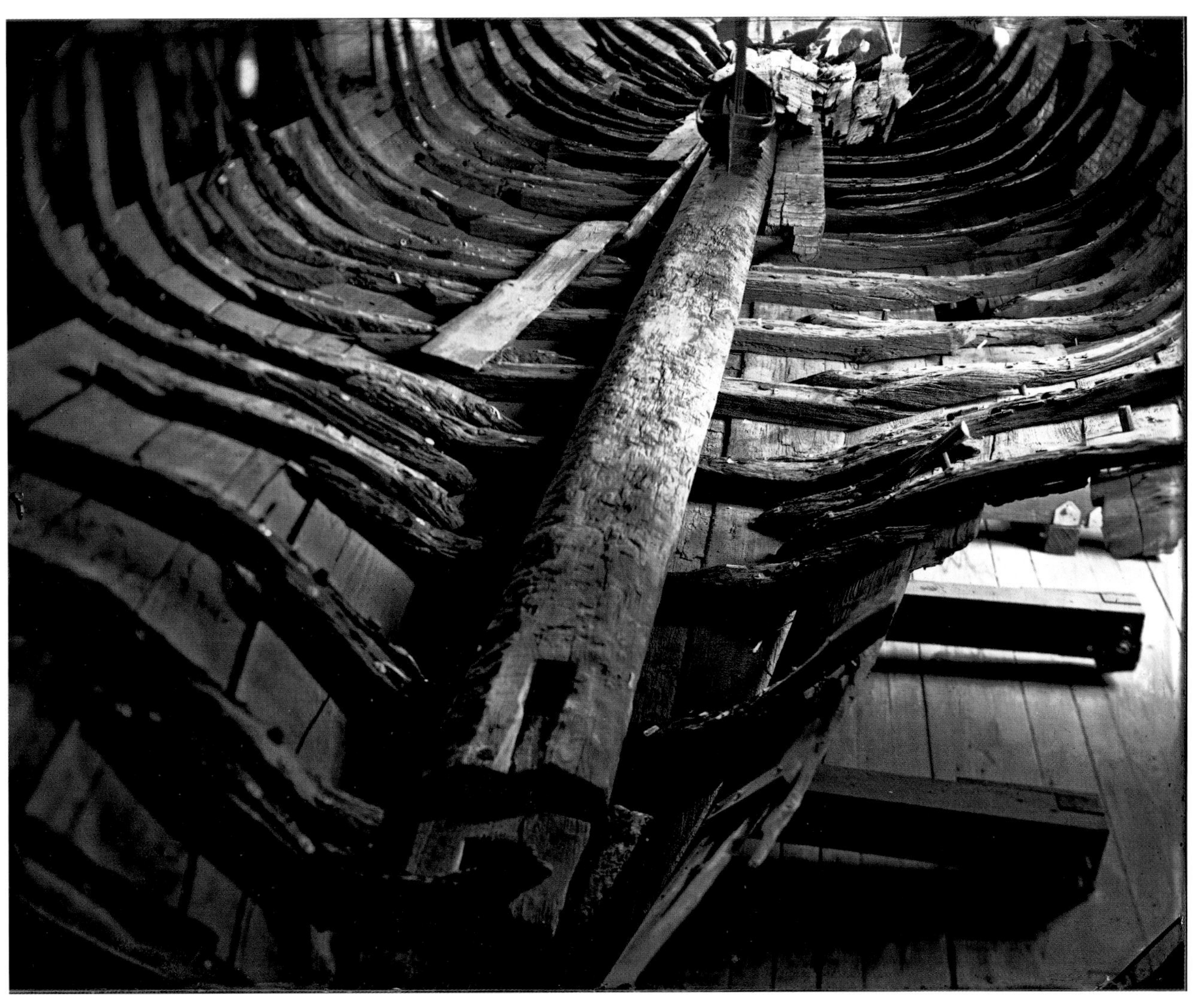

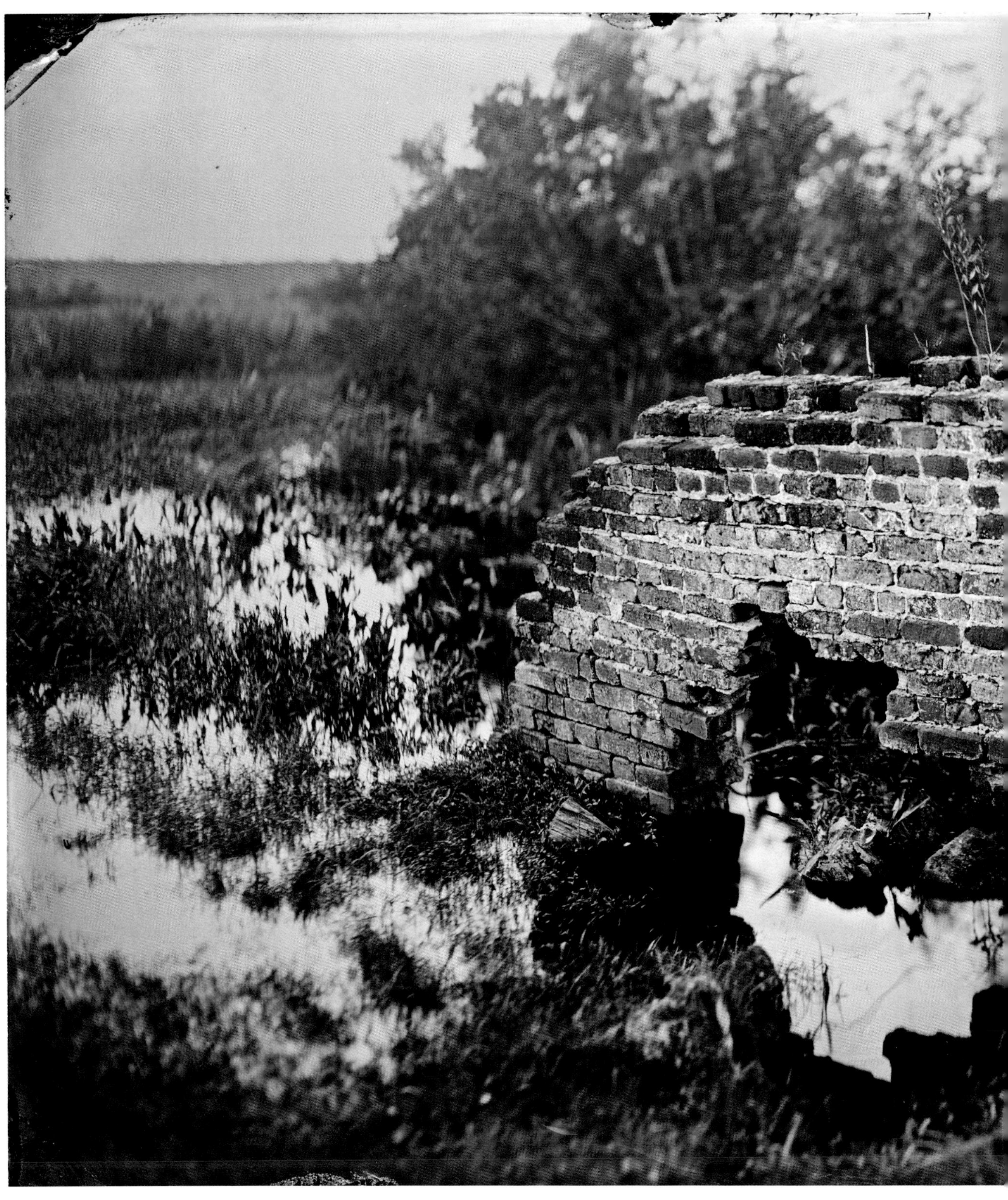

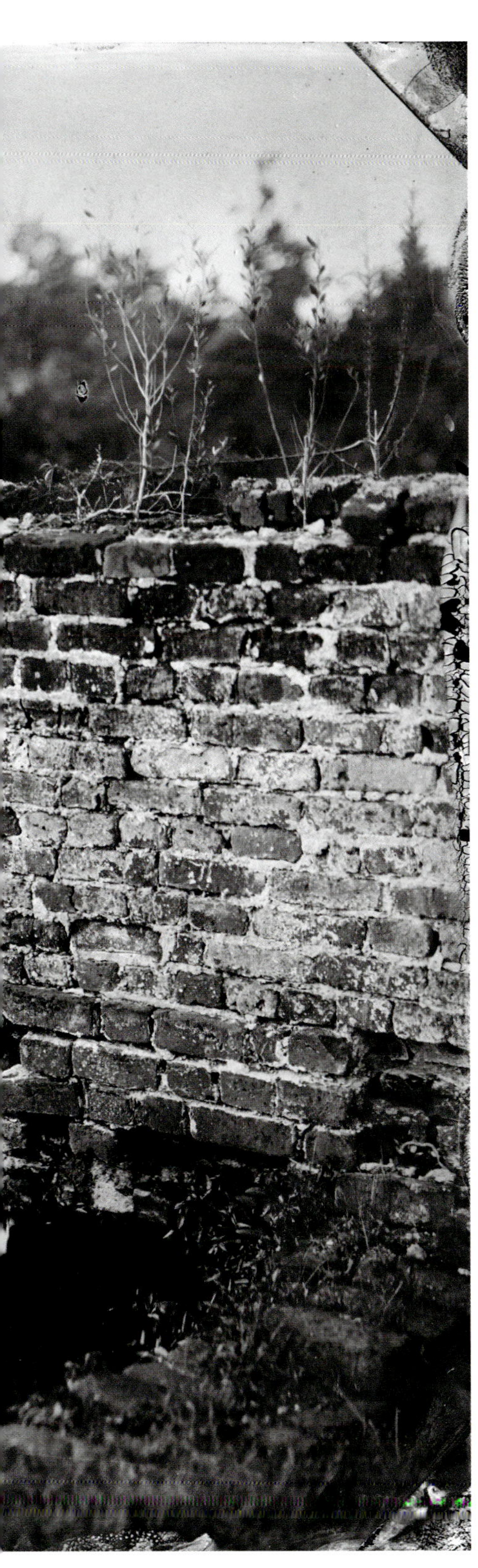

RICE MILL RUIN, MIDDLEBURG PLANTATION
At high tide, this wall becomes surrounded by water. It is the only structure left of a two-story warehouse and rice mill dating from the 1800s and early 1900s.

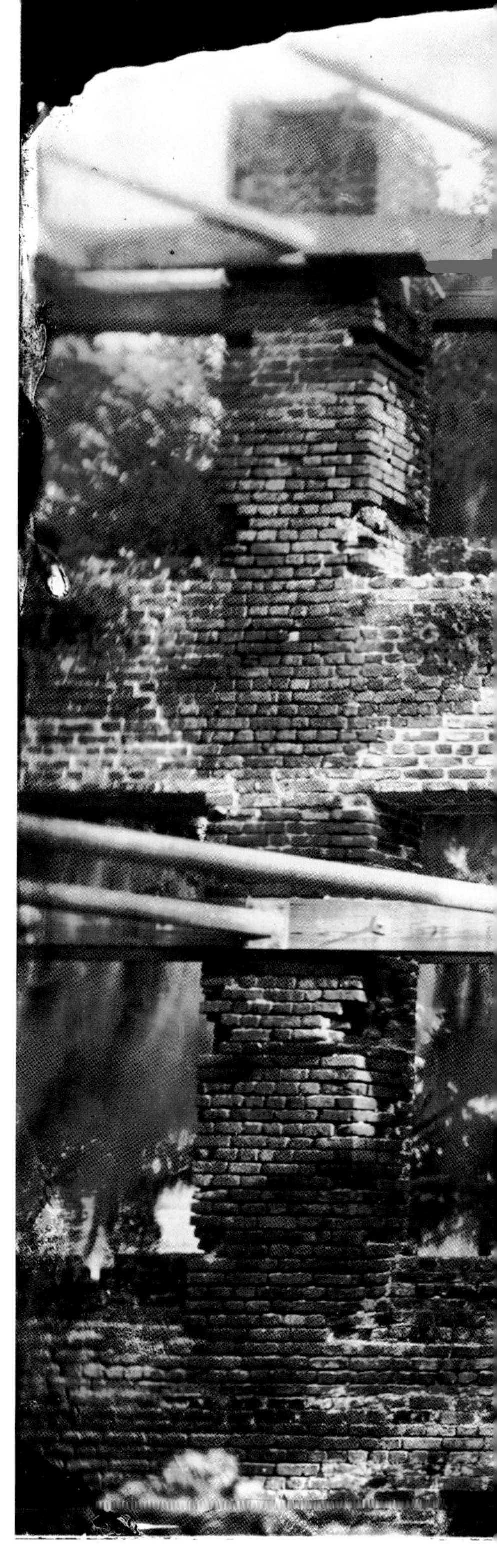

WITNESS TREE, RUSSELL CREEK, EDISTO ISLAND
Witness tree stands beside the Brick House ruin, a colonial dwelling built in 1725. In the early 1700s, prosperous Europeans in the Lowcountry began shipping rice, cotton, and indigo from Edisto Island to Charleston's wharfs on the Inner Passage.

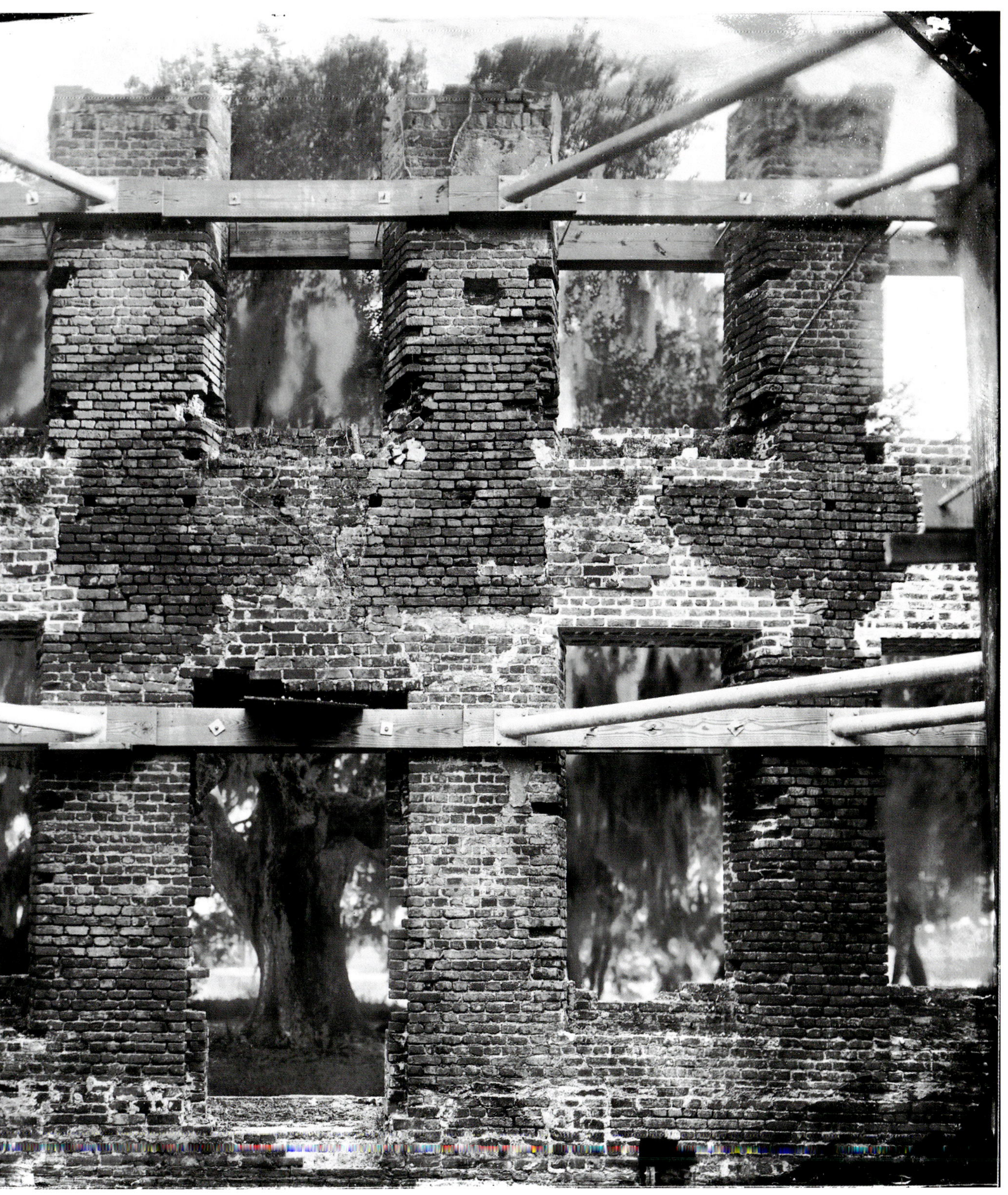

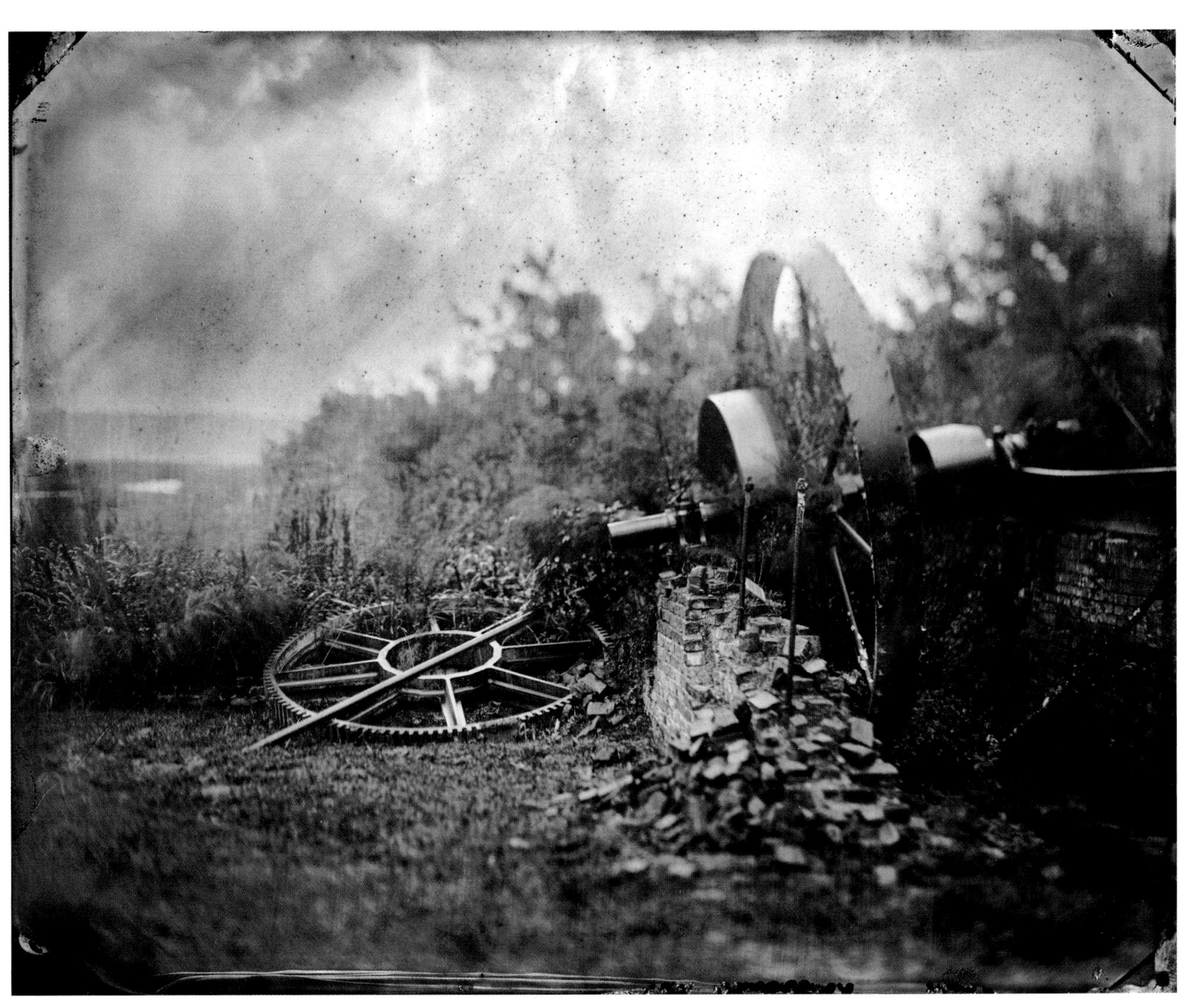

RICE MILLING WHEEL, COOPER RIVER
Iron wheels from the first toll rice mill remain beside the Cooper River. The two-story milling house has been dismantled, and only a portion of its brick wall is visible.

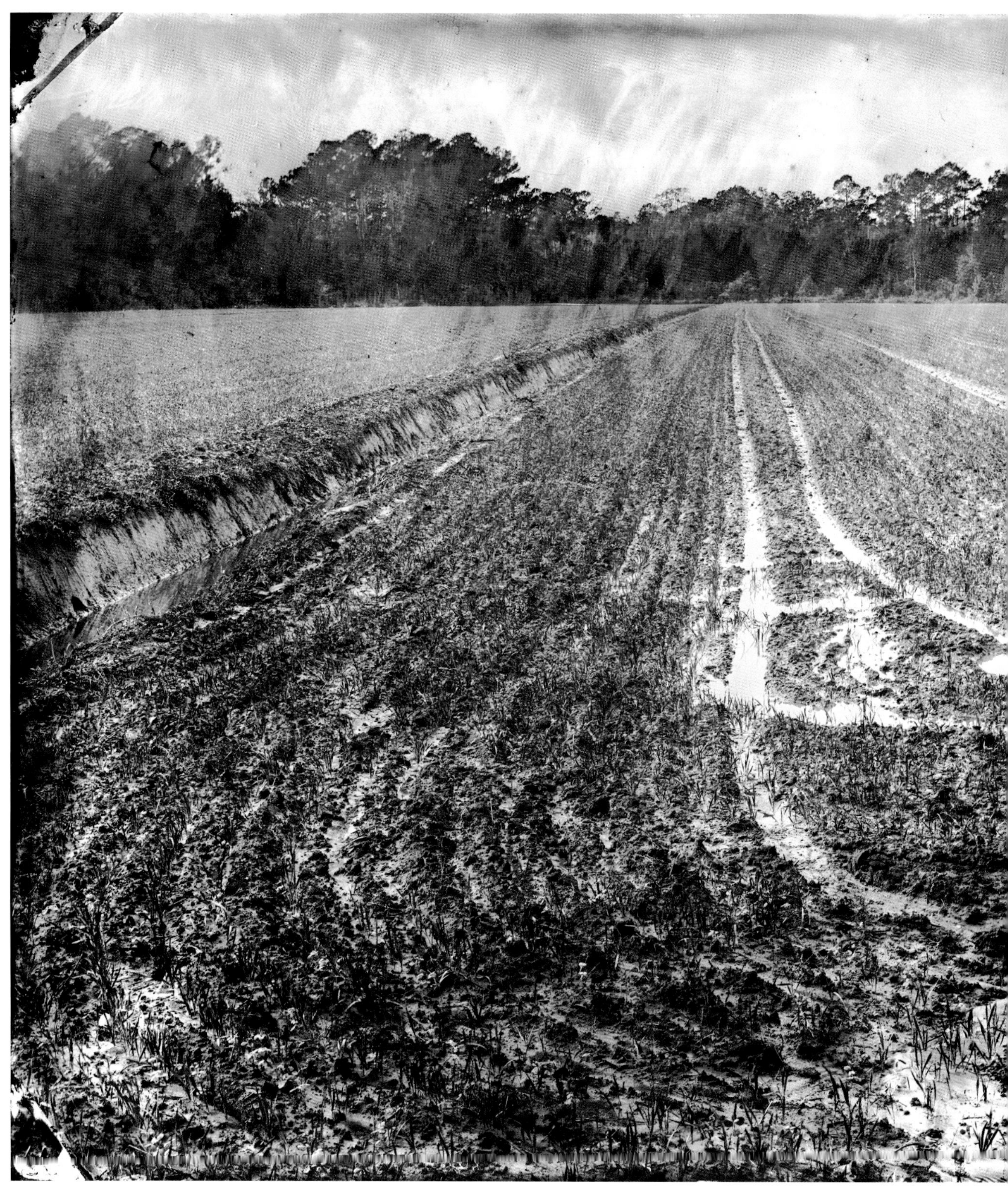

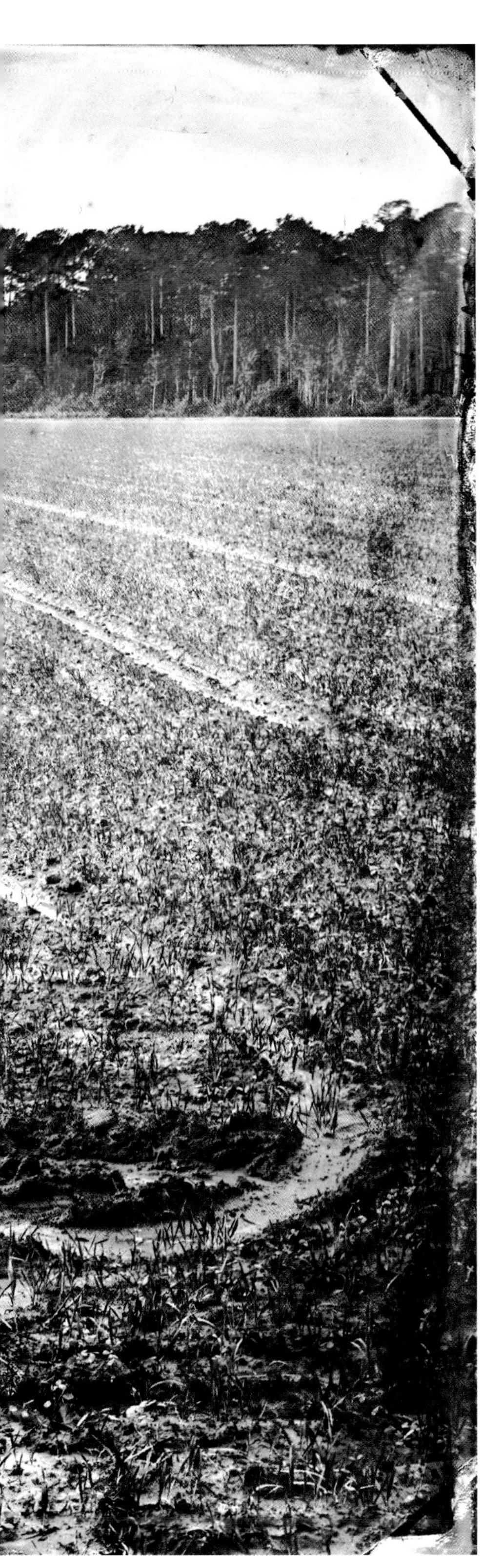

ANCIENT FIELD, BUGBY PLANTATION,
WADMALAW ISLAND
Archival land plats indicate that Europeans began cultivating this field on Bohicket Creek for agriculture in the 1700s. Fields in the Lowcountry are at sea level and hold rain water for days.

BRICK CHIMNEY FOR RICE MILLING, MIDDLEBURG PLANTATION

A seventy-five-foot-tall brick chimney is one of the last intact structures from the first steam-powered rice mill built in South Carolina. Local planters brought their rice crops to the mill and paid a toll to process the rice before it was loaded onto boats and sent to Charleston.

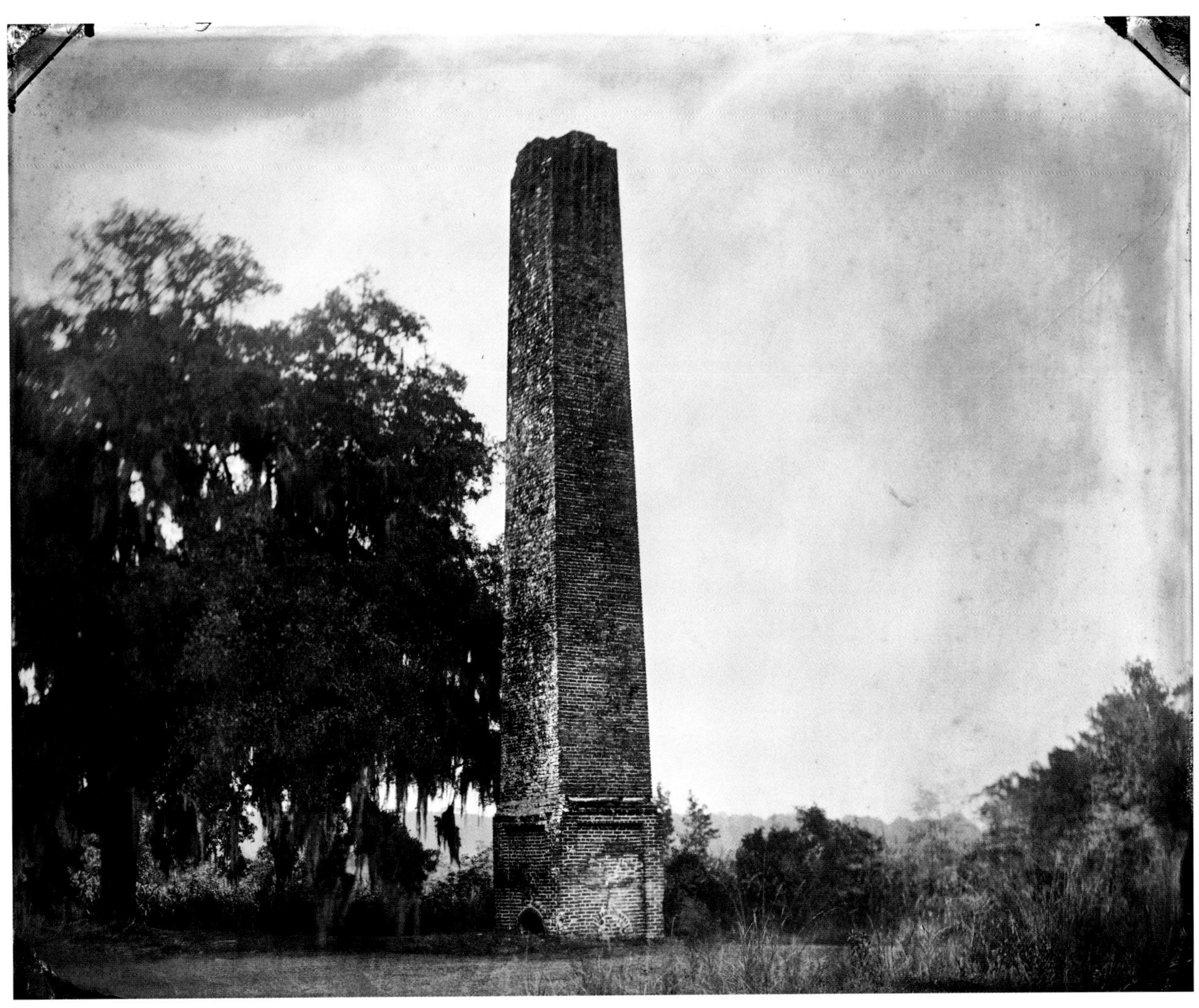

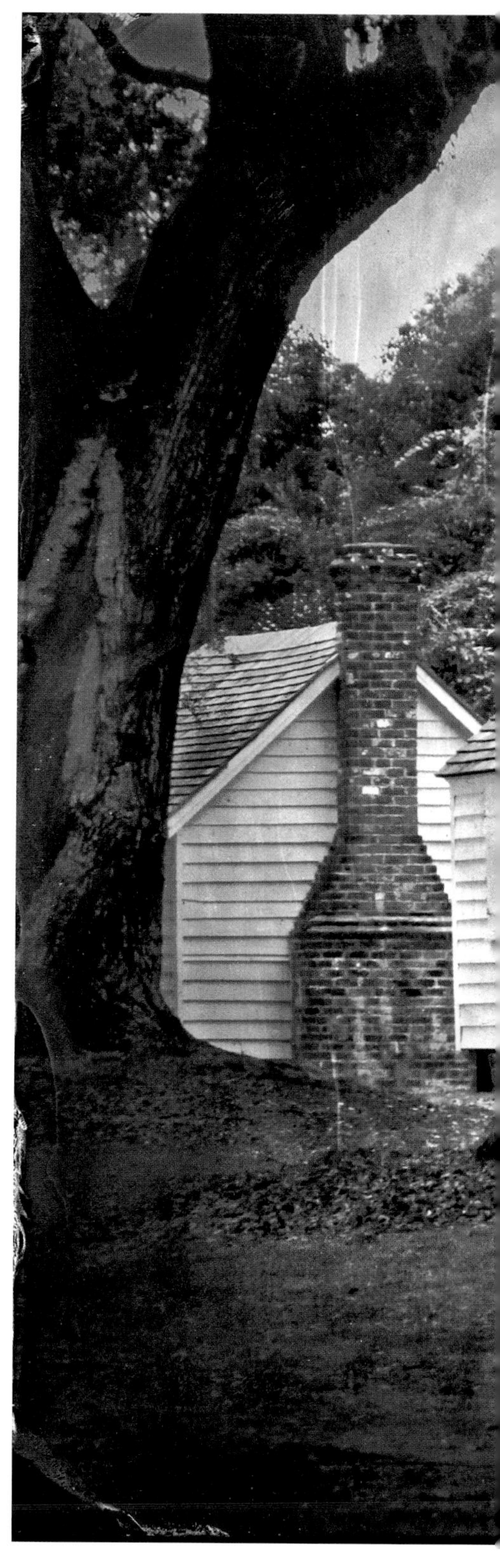

SLAVE CABINS, MCLEOD PLANTATION
Dating from the 1850s, these one-room dwellings beside Wappoo Cut housed enslaved laborers at McLeod and then their descendants for over a hundred years. Black people lived in the cabins until the 1980s.

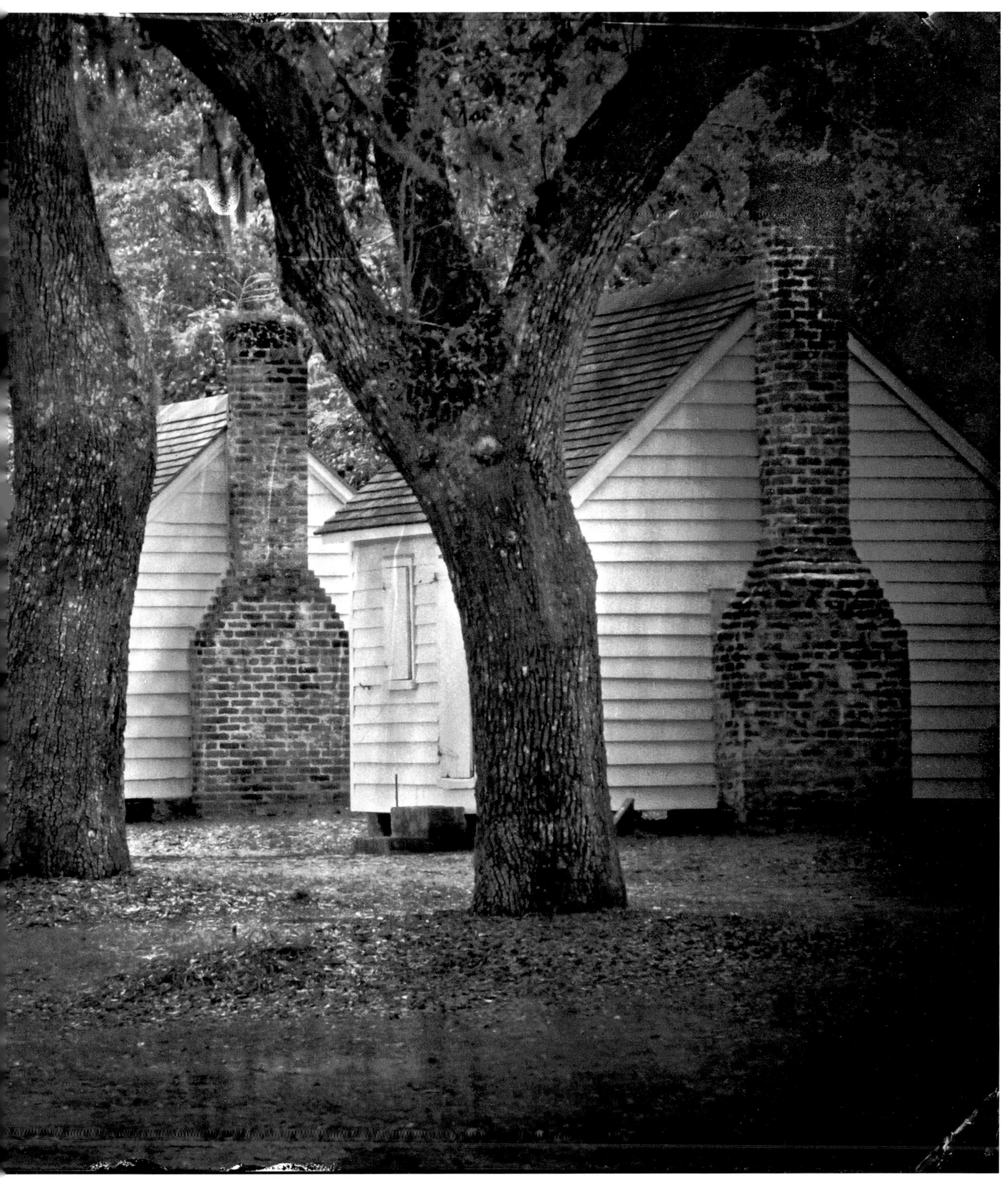

KENNETH L. MACK SR., WADMALAW ISLAND
Kenneth Mack is a dockworker at a marina on the Inner Passage. The Mack family has lived on Wadmalaw Island for centuries and includes hundreds of descendants who live nearby.

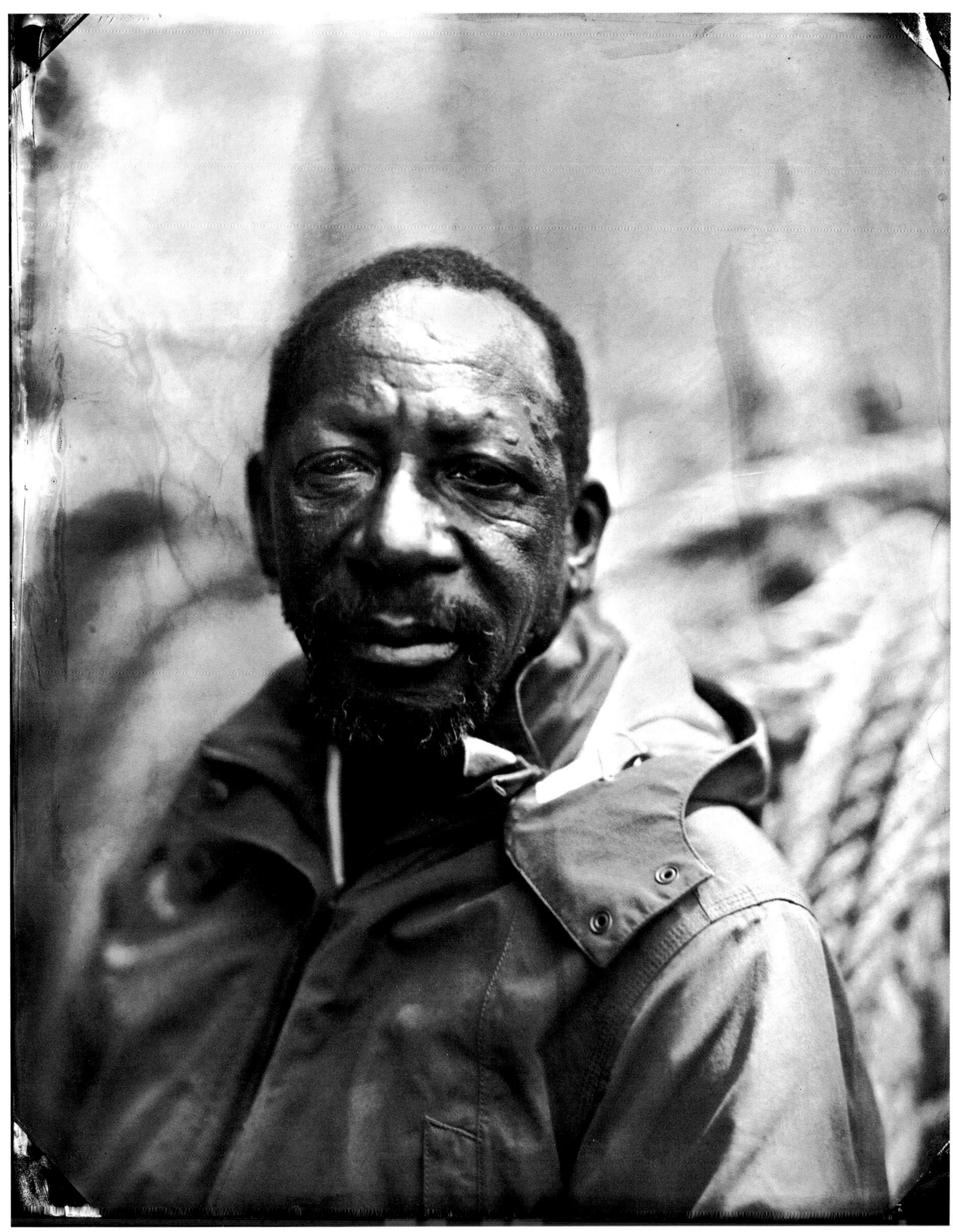

My brother still knows the water channels, but I don't anymore.

The girly part of growing up, I didn't care about that. That's the part that my grandmother, she tried so hard to teach me. How to do the canning and how to make the poke. But I don't know why I didn't like making the sweet potato pies that grandmother would try to teach me. I would just go off with the guys and go out on the water and do some fishing. That's my part. We fished in the Lowcountry rivers off James Island. I've always lived on right next to the water. I can walk to the river from our house. My brother still knows the water channels, but I don't anymore. I go with him now when I fish because I'll get lost in the creeks.

KATHY FLUDD HOLMES, JAMES ISLAND
Kathy Holmes traces her lineage back over six generations to Molly Fludd, who was born in 1830 on James Island. Every year, the Fludd family hosts a reunion that draws over two hundred descendants of Molly Fludd back to James Island.

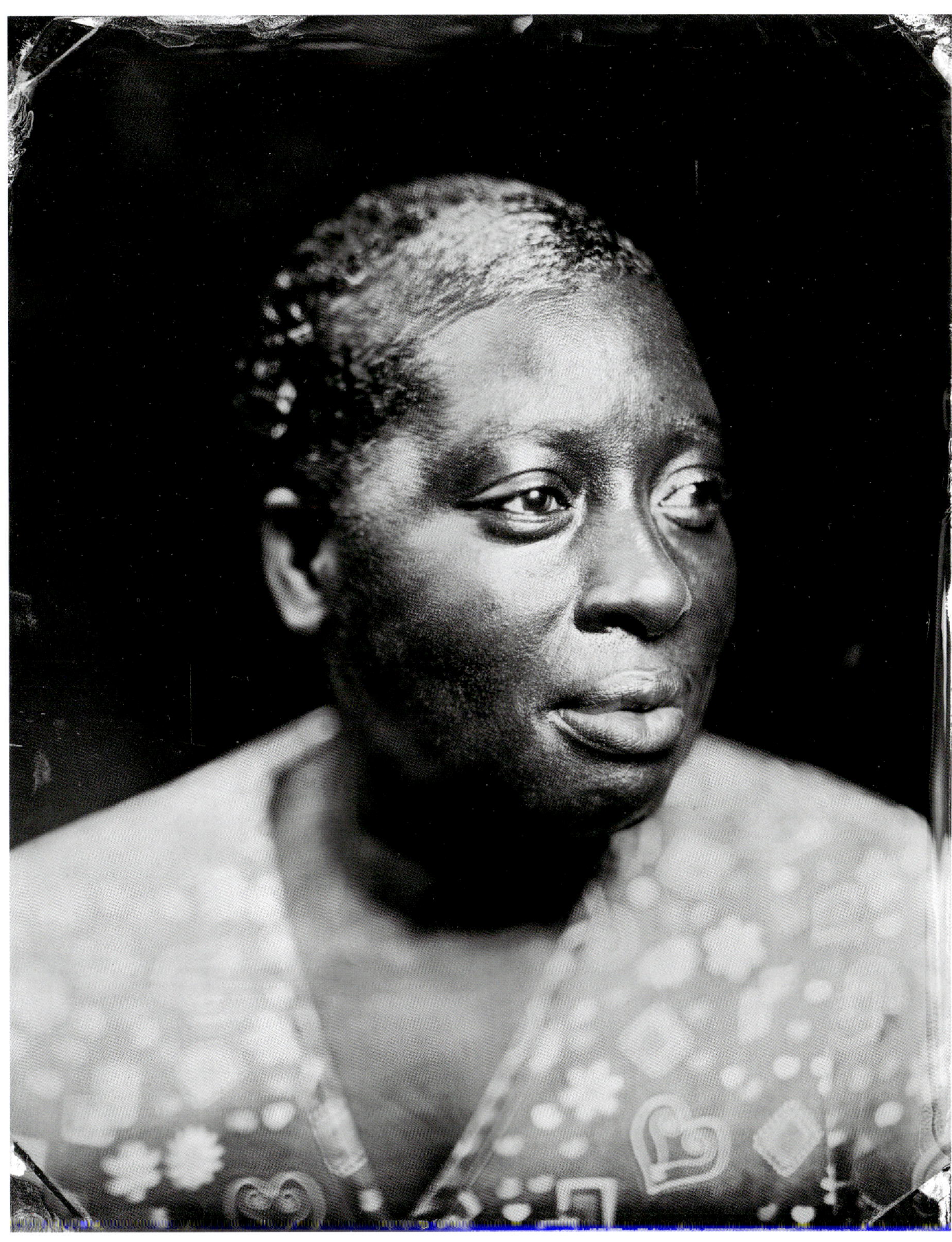

My home is tidal, a place that moves so quickly between shocking beauty and loric violence that it'll snatch the very breath from your lungs.

To truly understand the South Carolina Lowcountry, you have to experience it by boat. There's something about leaving the land behind, wandering the endless waterways and marsh creeks, the salt on the air. It's magic. And like all magic, it both heals and destroys. Here we share a common cuisine, common music, a common pace to our lives. But we share, too, a cruel and heartbreaking history. It's why the Lowcountry is a place I am simultaneously ashamed of and endlessly proud of. My home is tidal, a place that moves so quickly between shocking beauty and loric violence that it'll snatch the very breath from your lungs.

RUTLEDGE HAMMES, NORTH CHARLESTON
Rutledge Hammes, a native Charlestonian and author, continues to be inspired by the Gullah Geechee stories his grandmother told him as a young boy. His ancestors arrived by boat from England in the late 1600s.

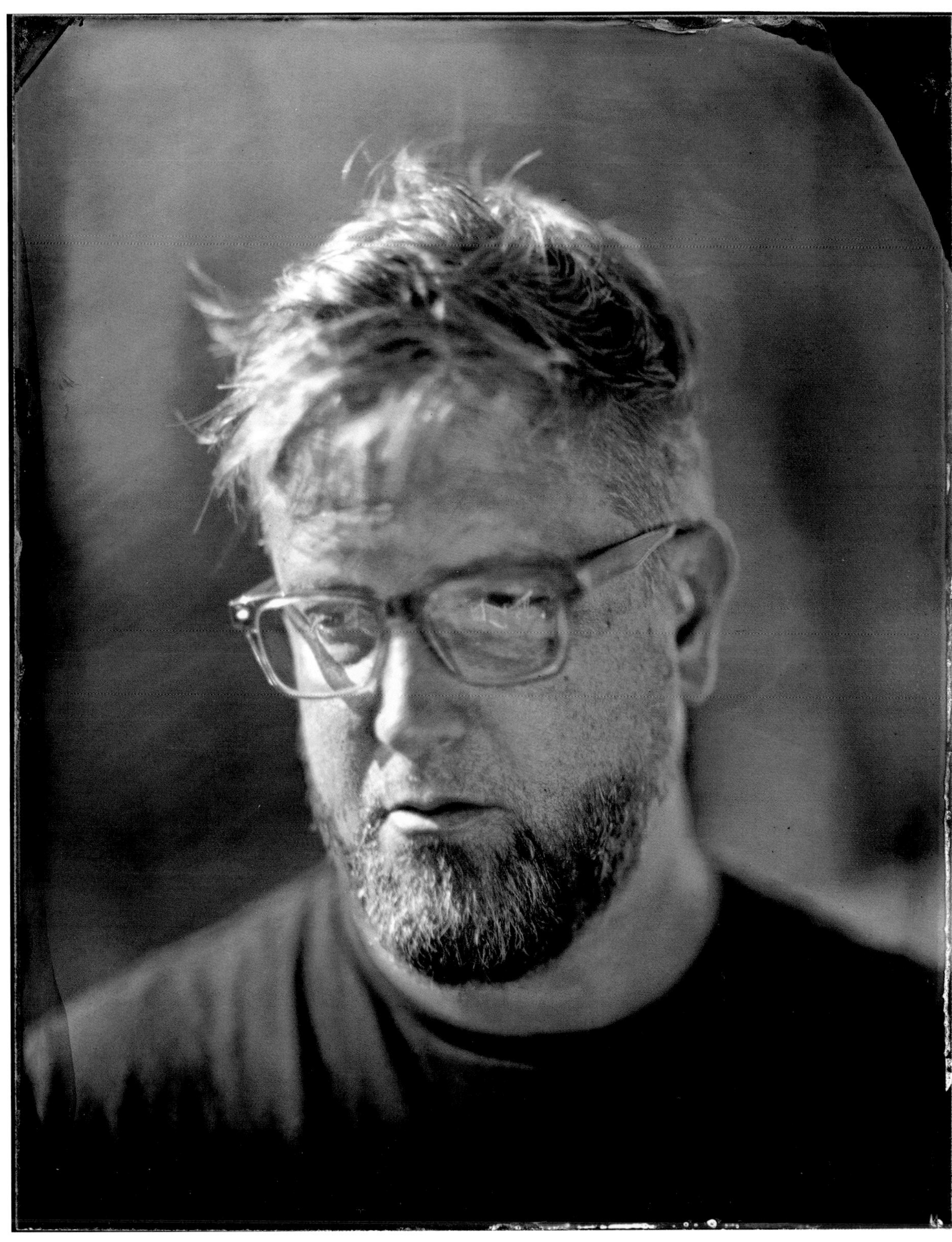

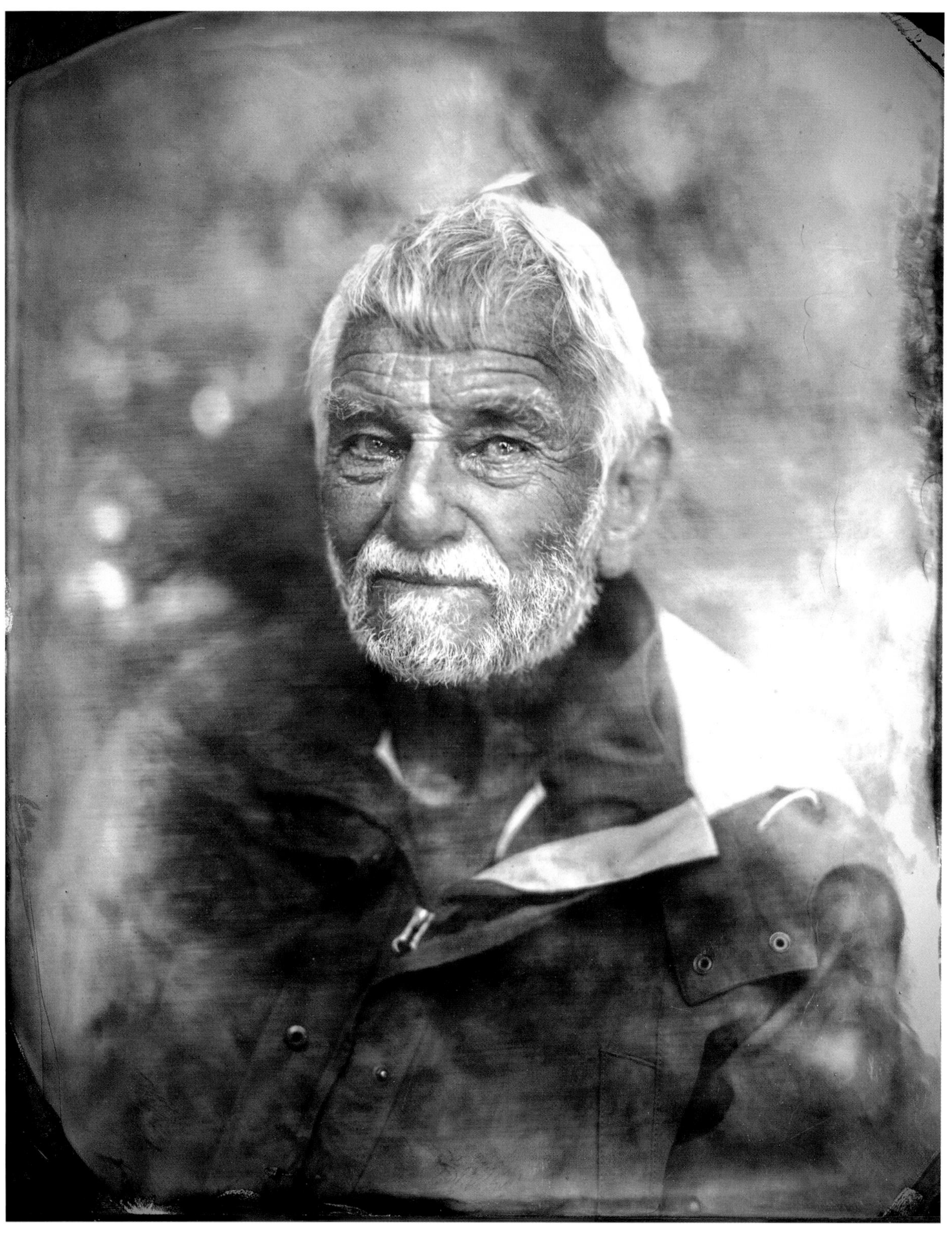

My uncle navigated through the rivers and creeks using a piecemeal map.

As a boy growing up on Wadmalaw Island, my uncle let me pilot a barge that traveled through the inland rivers and creeks. The first time I drove the boat, I misjudged a turn and grounded our barge on a sandbar. We had to wait until high tide for the water to come in and free us. My uncle navigated through the rivers and creeks using a piecemeal map of the water route from Edisto to Charleston. He constructed the map himself by taping pieces of old river charts together in a long strip. I still have that map.

MICAH JOHN LAROCHE III, WADMALAW ISLAND
Micah LaRoche worked as a waterman for decades and navigated a barge on the Inner Passage by "counting Lowcountry creeks," a technique he learned from his uncle who also worked as a boatman. LaRoche's family has lived on the Sea Islands of South Carolina since the 1700s.

I connect with the ancestors, whose voices speak to me all the time, by cooking food that has been lost.

I connect with the ancestors, whose voices speak to me all the time, by cooking food that has been lost, making recipes that are accessible only from Gullah Geechee ancestors like my grandfather. When I cook, I am interested in reaching the place where Senegal meets Gullah.

BENJAMIN DENNIS, RIDGELAND, SOUTH CAROLINA
Benjamin "B. J." Dennis, an acclaimed chef who was born and raised in Charleston, cooks traditional Lowcountry meals inspired by his Gullah Geechee heritage.

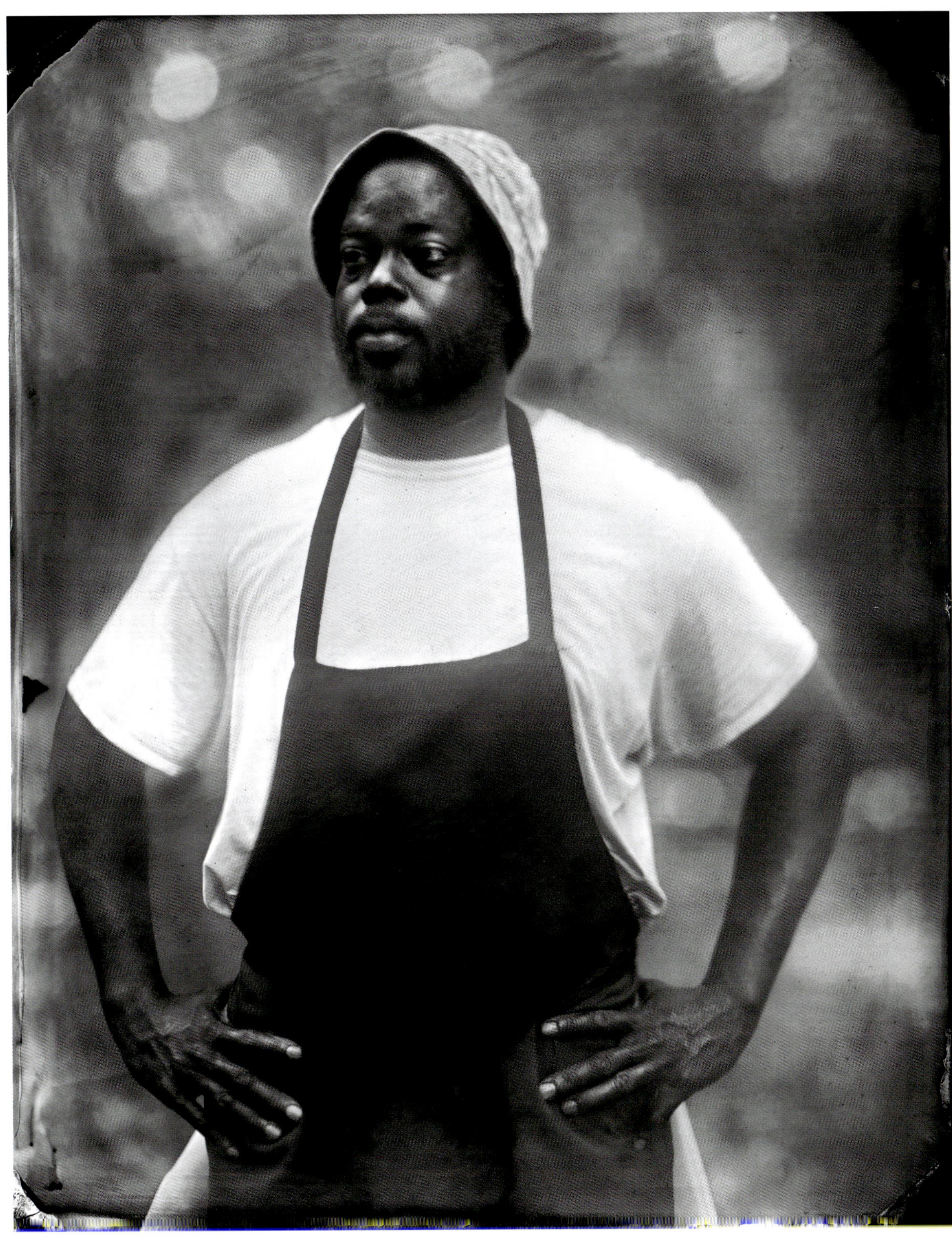

ANILENA HAMMES, NORTH CHARLESTON

Anilena Hammes, three years old, is a native Charlestonian. Her ancestors, the Middletons and the Heywards, arrived in the Lowcountry in 1683 and were later signers of the Declaration of Independence. Three generations of her family still live in the Lowcountry.

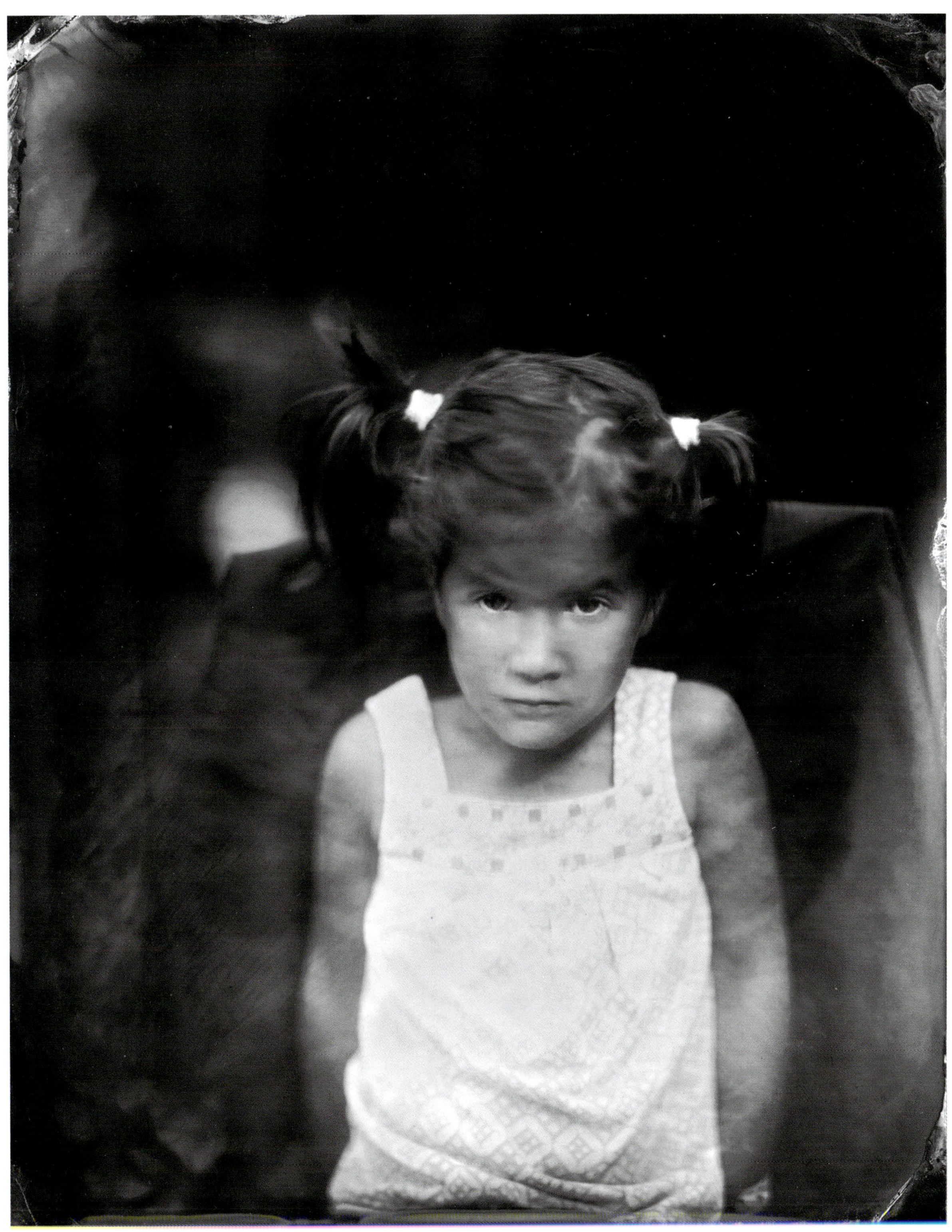

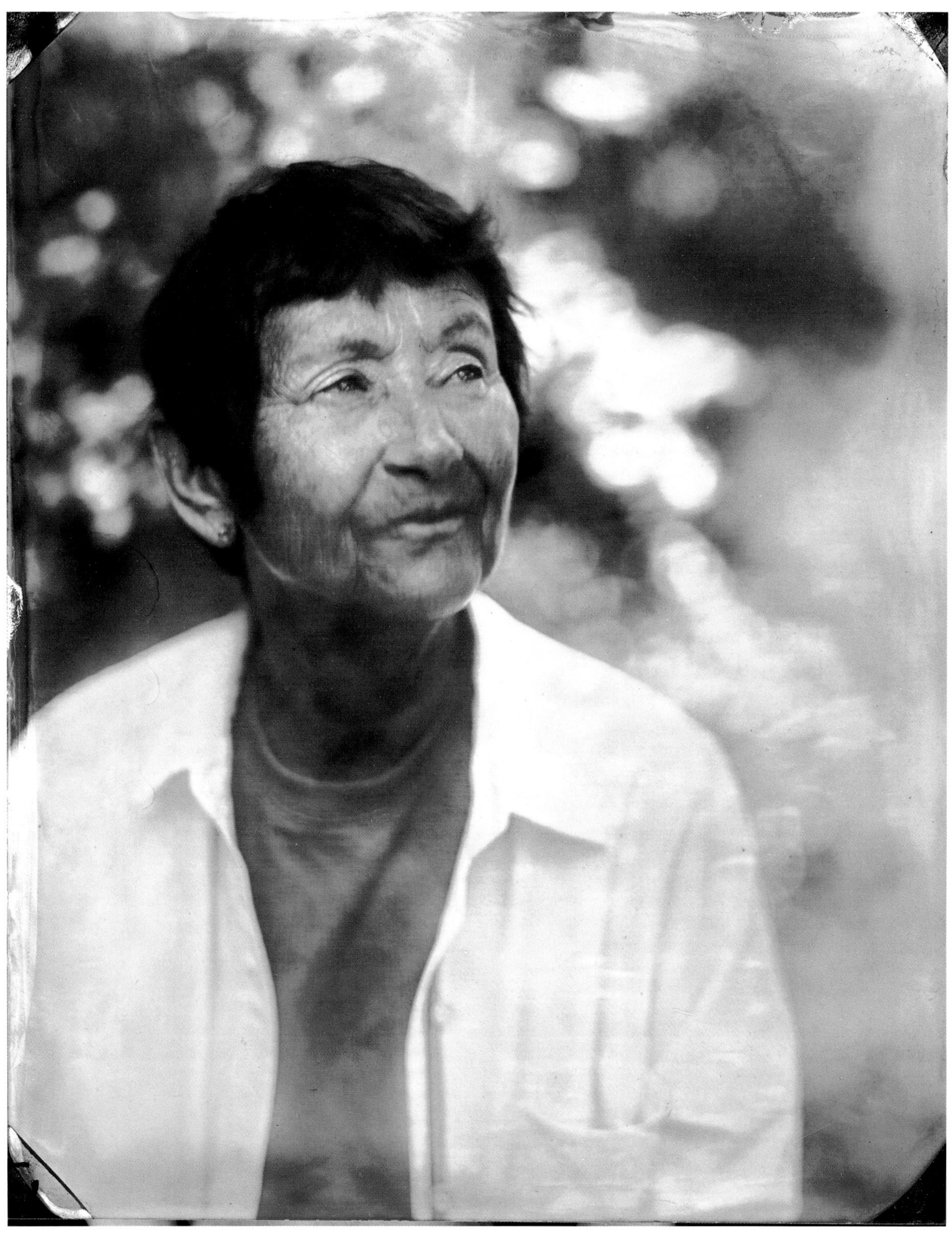

JANE LAROCHE, WADMALAW ISLAND
LaRoche raised her family in the village of Rockville, a town noted on seventeenth-century maps as "Rock" on "Indian lands."

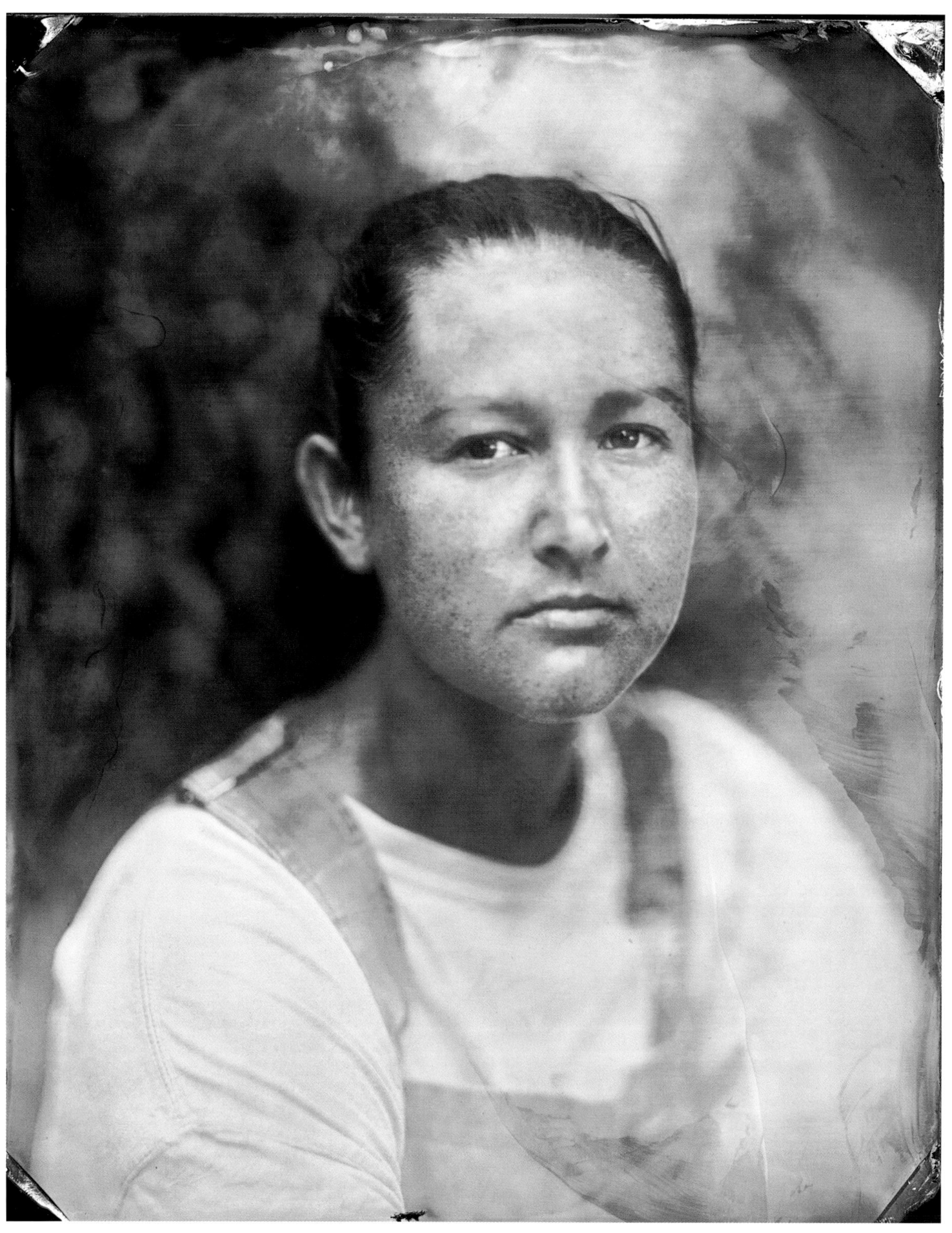

No whistling, for fear you'll whistle up a storm.

There are lots of superstitions about fishing that are still observed in our fleet of boats moored on Wadmalaw Island. You never leave on a Friday. No cats on the boat. No women on the boat. No bananas. No fruit on the boat at all. The fishermen once said "no breasts." No pigs on board. No whistling, for fear you'll whistle up a storm. Any sort of pork on a vessel is bad luck. But Todd, one of the fishermen, has a pot-bellied pig that goes out to sea fishing with him.

OLIVIA LAROCHE CONDON, SUMMERVILLE, SOUTH CAROLINA
For over a hundred years, Olivia Condon's family has run a fishing business on the Inner Passage. Her ancestors have navigated the waterway since the 1800s

Our history, Black history, is still here in the land.

My roots in the South extend from Alabama to Kentucky, including Virginia, the Carolinas, Tennessee. When I go back and set foot on the ground where my ancestors lived, whether it's in Tennessee or at a family reunion in Warrenton, North Carolina, I am connecting with the power of my past. It's a way of paying homage and saying that I see you to my people. Their life was not in vain. It is appreciated. And because of my ancestors' selflessness, the community they created here in the South is where I feel at home. The church. Family homes. Agricultural lands. Cemeteries. Our history, Black history, is still here in the land.

FREDERICK MURPHY, THE CAROLINAS
Frederick Murphy traces his passion for Black history to a family photograph from the mid-1800s that depicts Isabelle Jones, a free woman of Cherokee descent, and her husband Amos, a formerly enslaved man with Creek lineage.

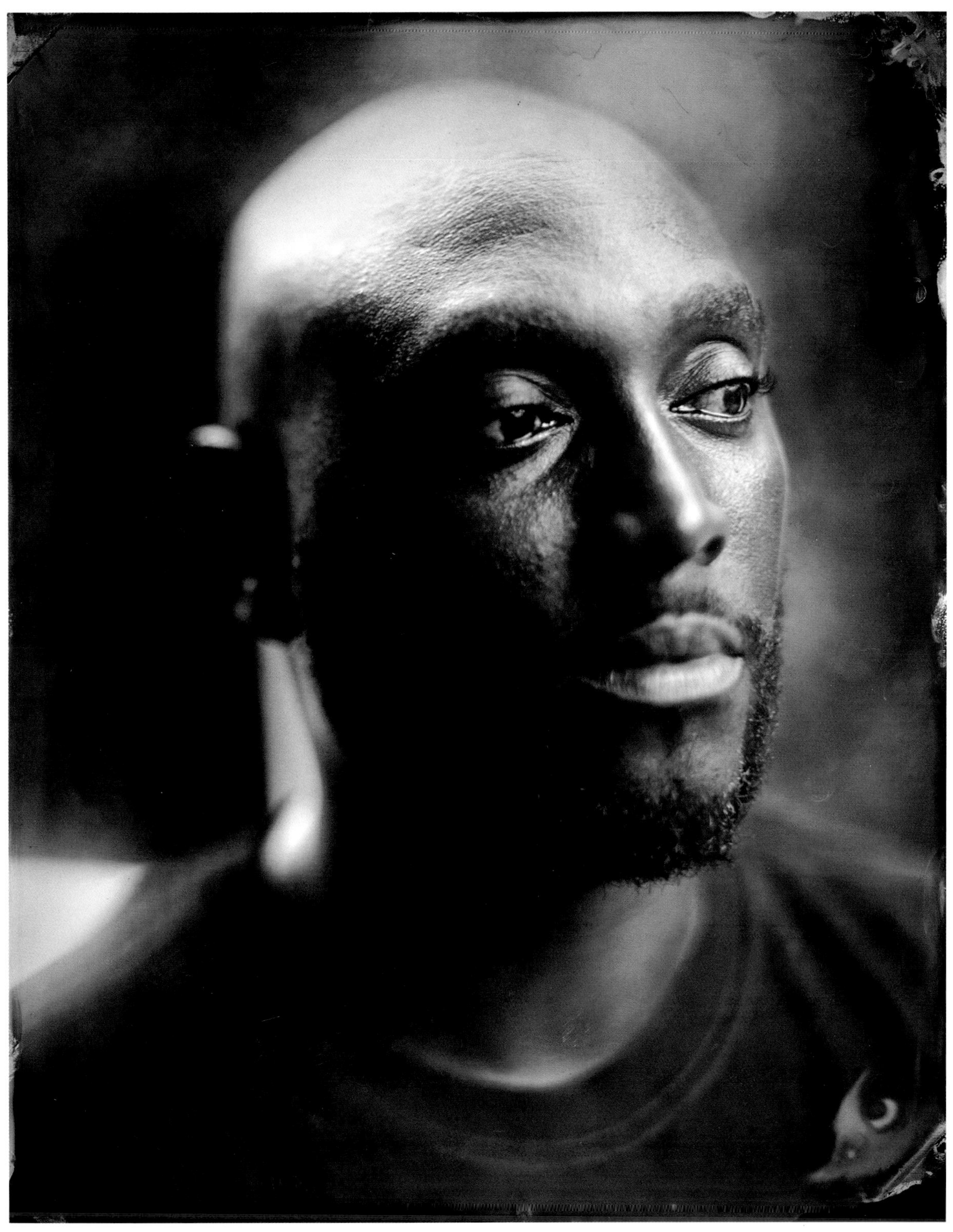

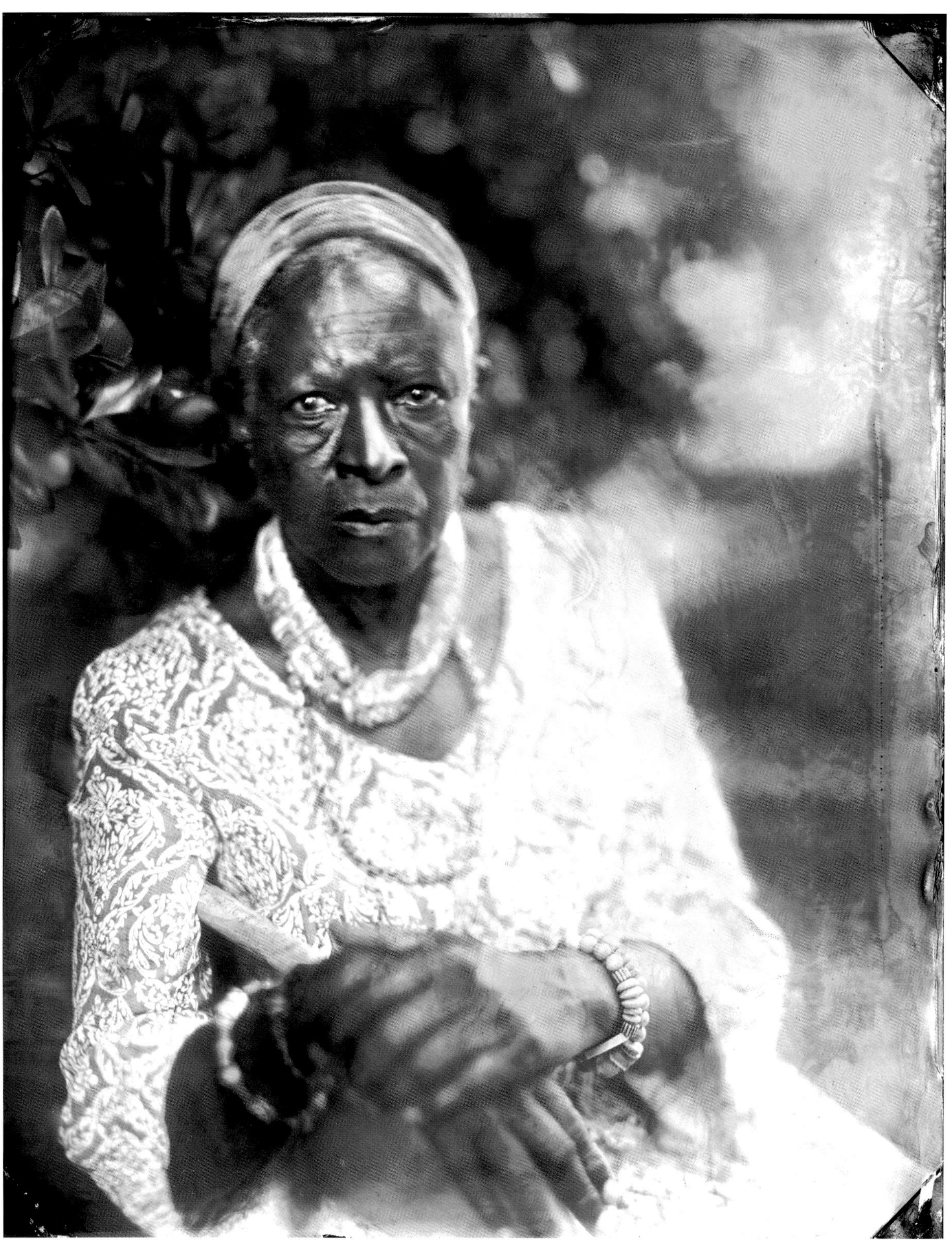

The Sea Islanders who still live there are descendants of the rice world.

The only way you can get to some of the coastal islands in South Carolina is by boat, leaving your car on the mainland. During the time of enslavement, Black workers cut a canal through the marsh between Sandy Island and the mainland, and even now everyone travels on a boat through that same canal to reach the island. The Sea Islanders who still live there are the descendants of the rice world.

VENNIE DEAS MOORE, GEORGETOWN
Vennie Deas Moore, a cultural historian and author, was born in the fishing village of Awendaw and raised in the city of Charleston. Her people have lived in the Lowcountry for generations; they include Africans, Europeans, Indigenous people, and Gullah Geechee.

JOHNO CREEK LEADS TO THE ASHEPOO RIVER
Planters used the tidal fresh water from Johno Creek to flood their rice fields. Wooden barges loaded with rice traveled the creek to reach the larger Ashepoo River and the routes of the Inner Passage.

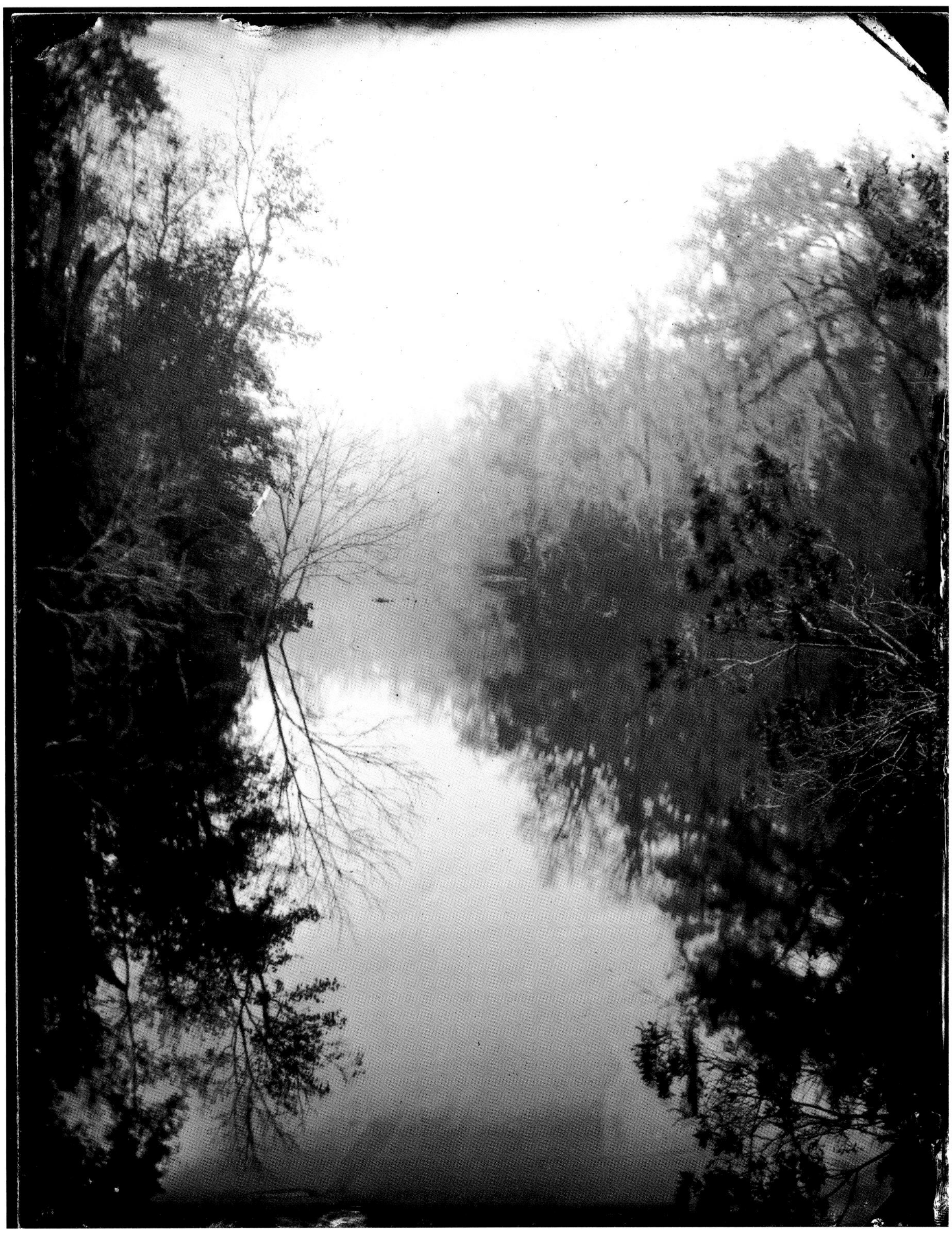

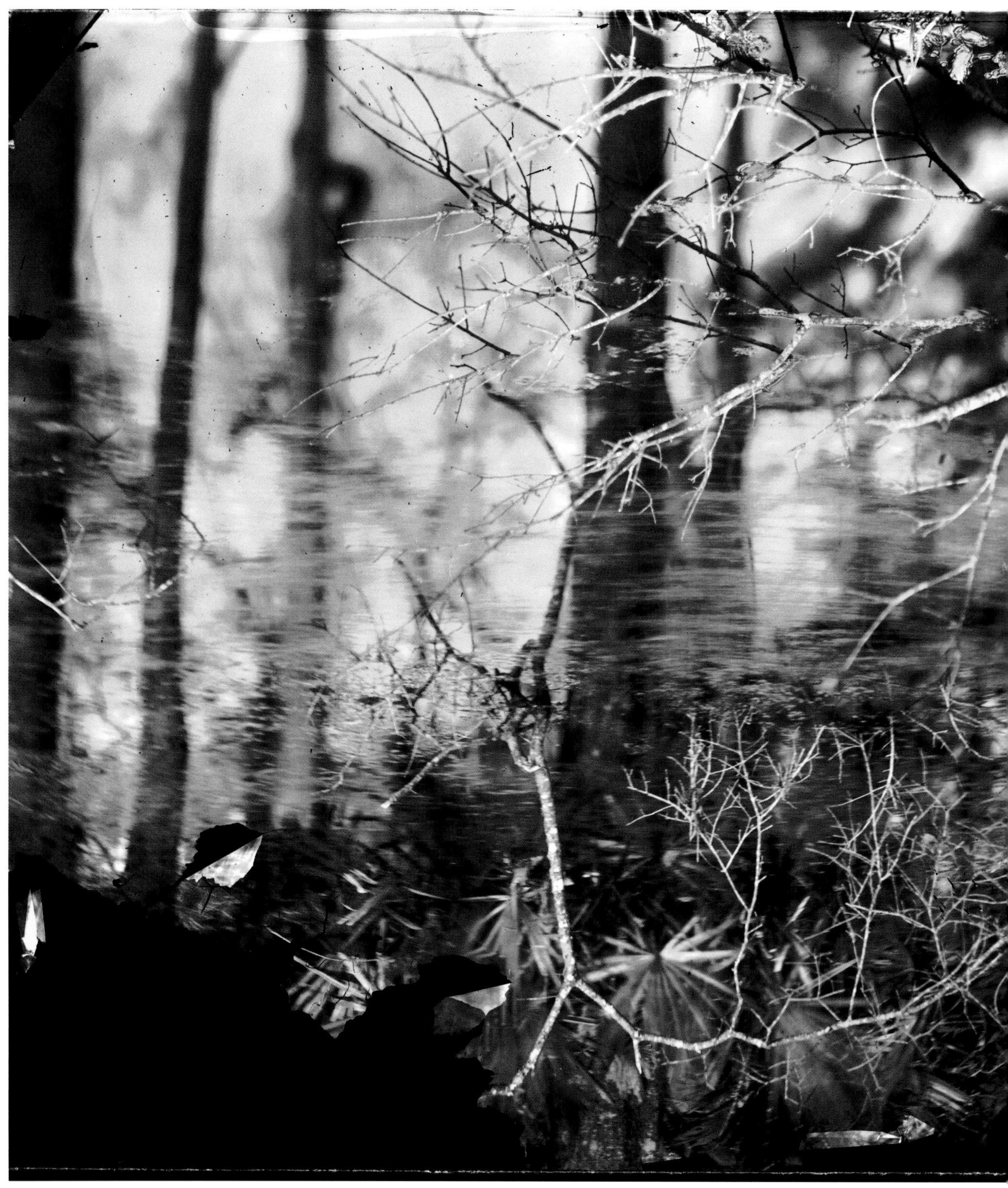

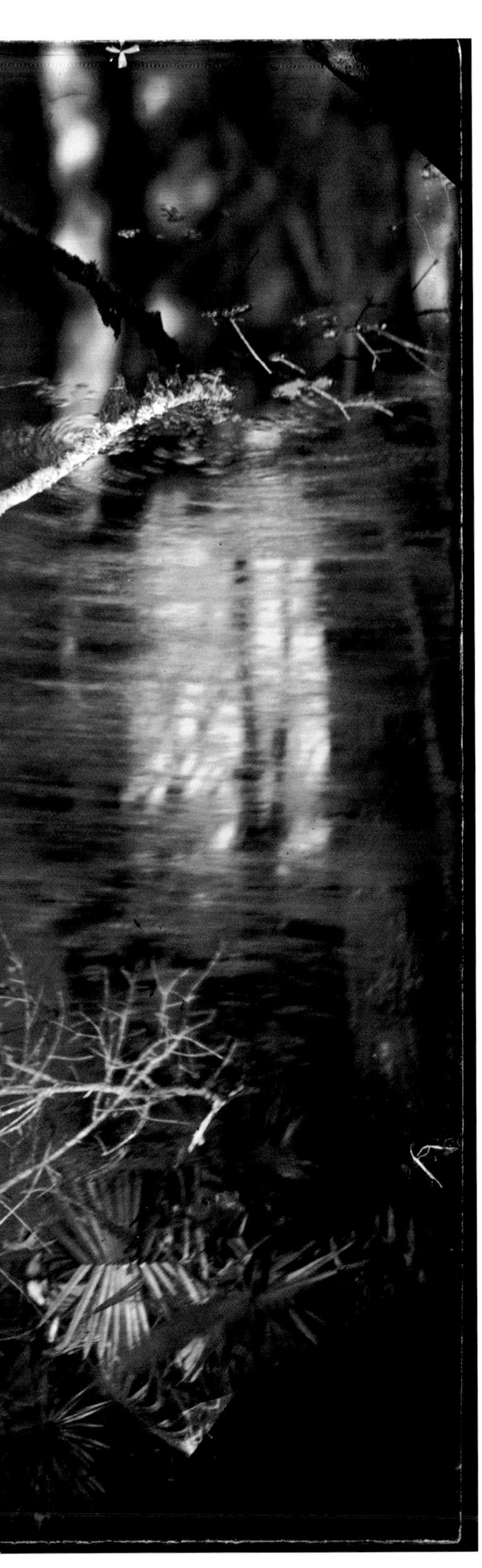

FLOODED FIELDS, COLLETON COUNTY
As the ocean flows inland, walkable paths disappear into watery estuaries under seven-foot tides. Travelers in the 1700s navigated boats through the Inner Passage rather than risk becoming mired in the few muddy footpaths that led to Charleston.

RICE CANAL, COLLETON COUNTY
Historic canal brought fresh water from the Combahee River to inland rice fields at a former plantation on the Inner Passage waterway.

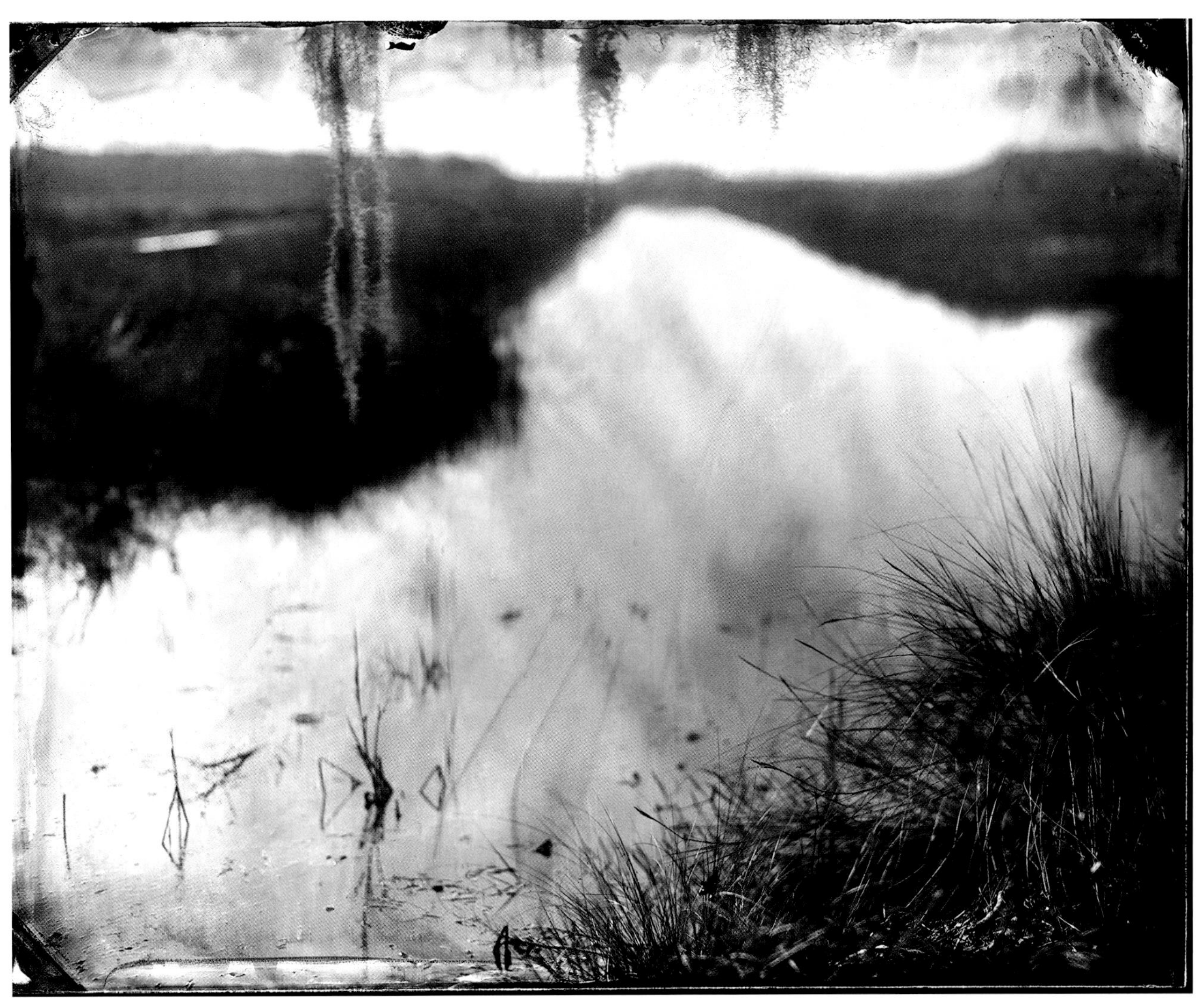

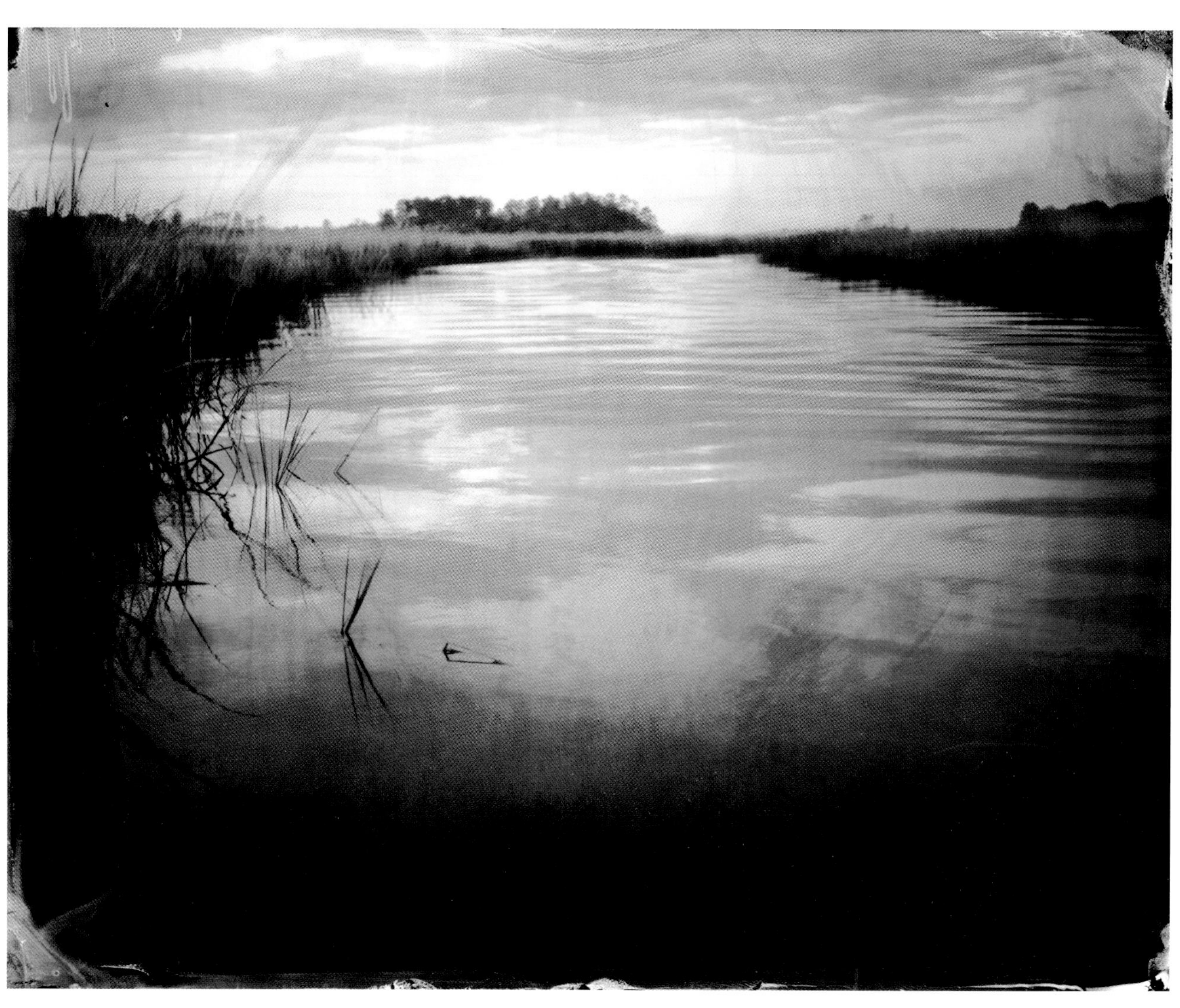

NEW CUT CANAL AT HIGH TIDE

In the early 1700s, the South Carolina Assembly conscripted enslaved and indentured men to dig a water channel six feet deep and ten feet wide. Boats carrying deerskins, pitch, tar, and later rice and indigo to Charleston's markets passed through New Cut.

EDISTO ISLAND, SOUTH CAROLINA
View of waterway on the Inner Passage from a former plantation on Edisto Island.

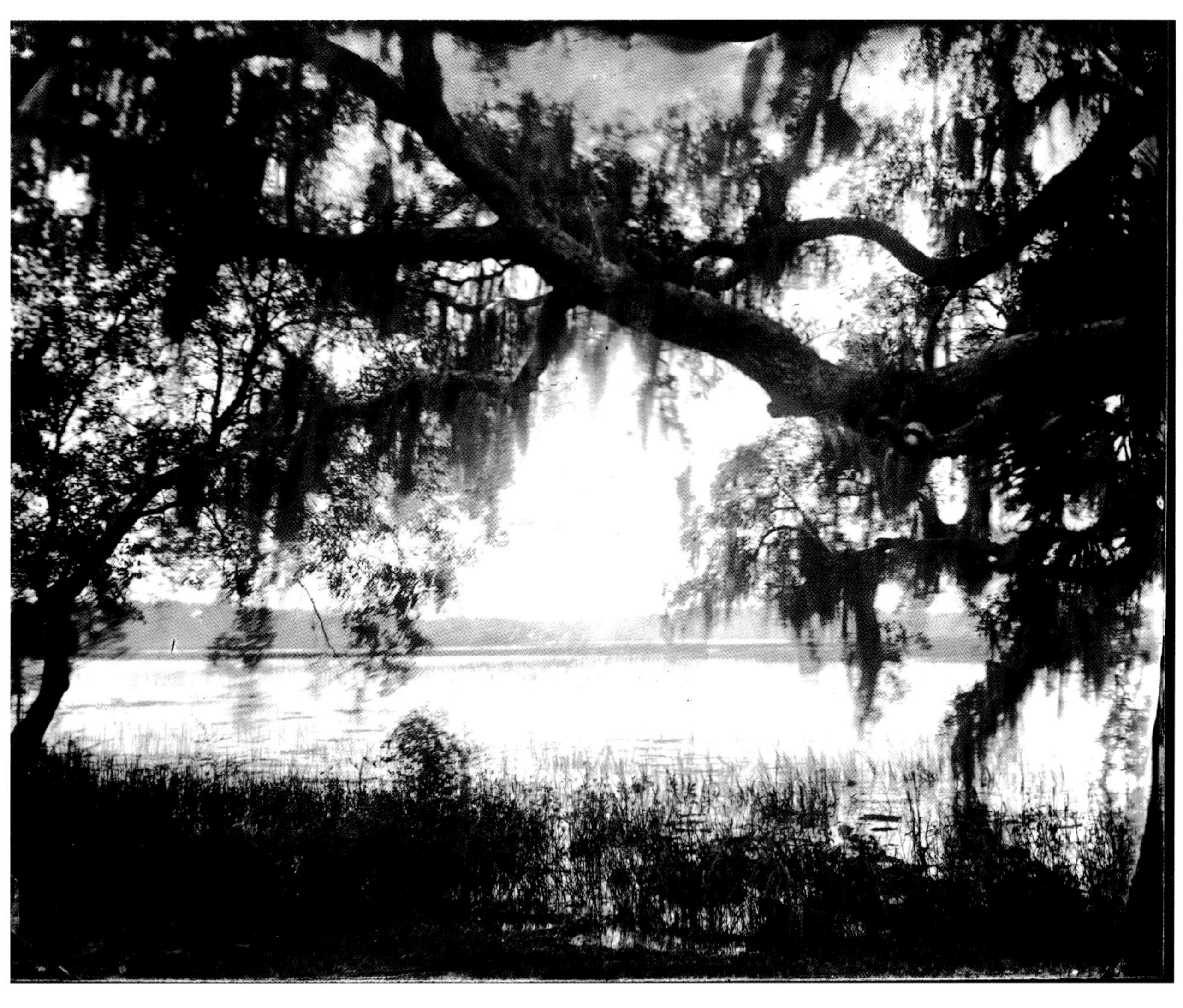

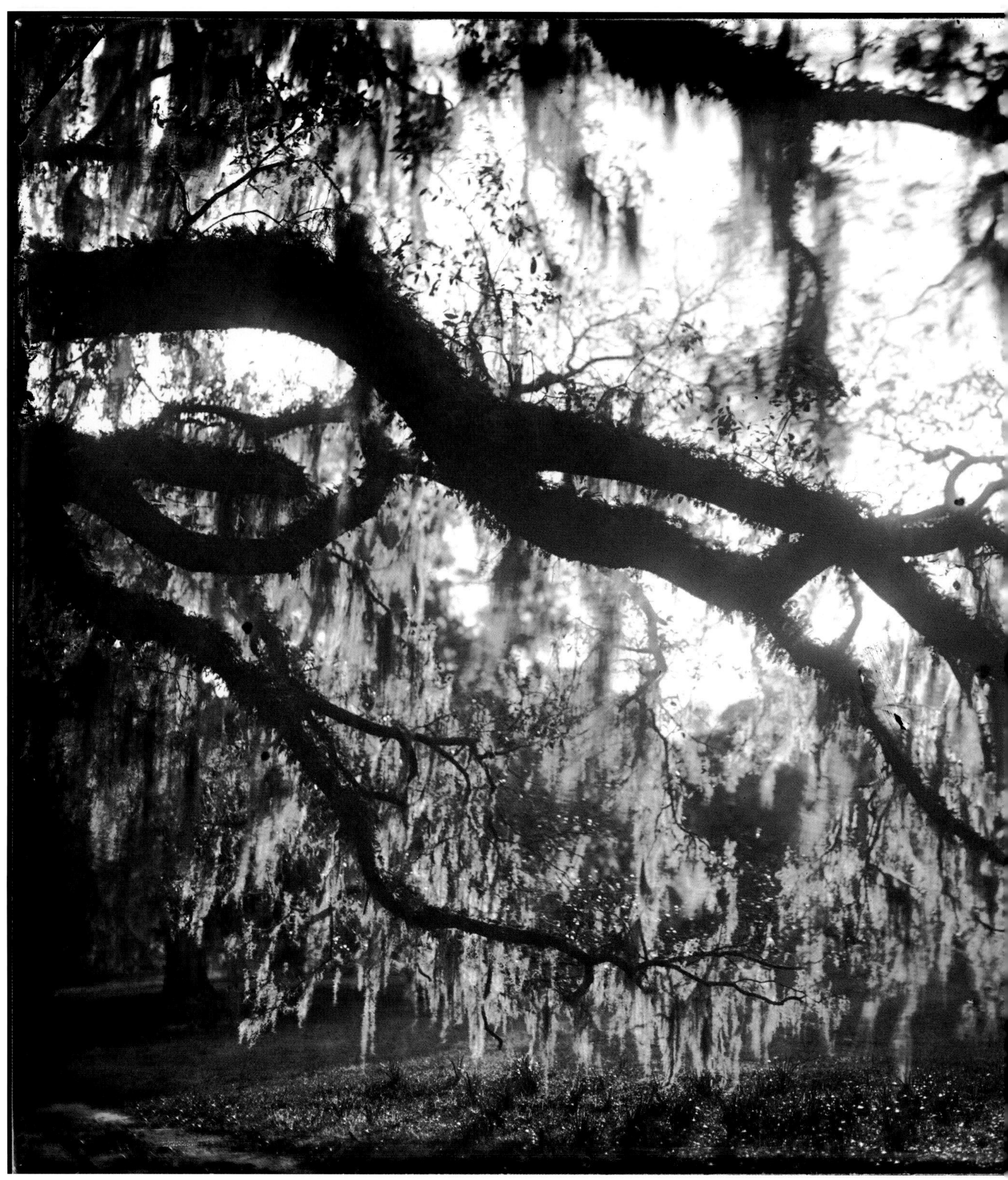

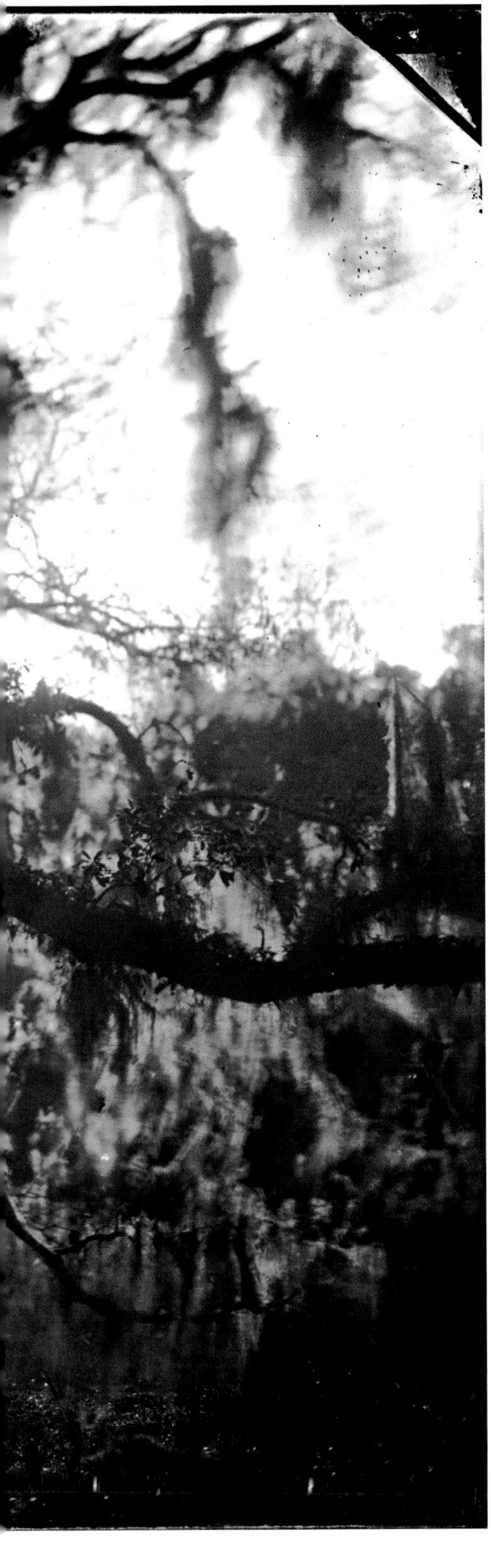

OAK TREE IN THE CHURCHYARD, WILLTOWN, SOUTH CAROLINA
Founded about 1704, Willtown or "New London" was an English settlement located on the South Edisto River. Settlers from Willtown traveled to Charleston on the Inner Passage.

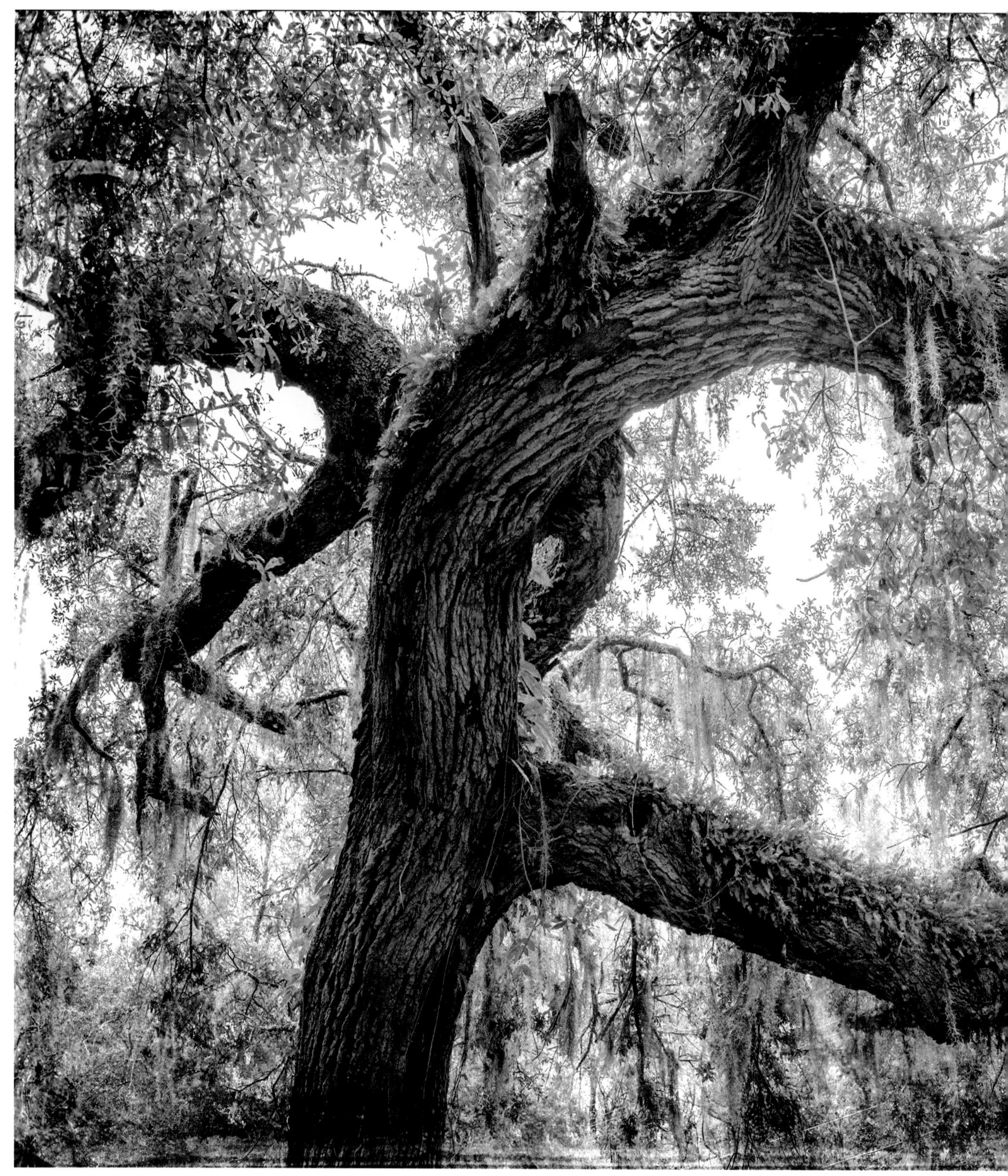

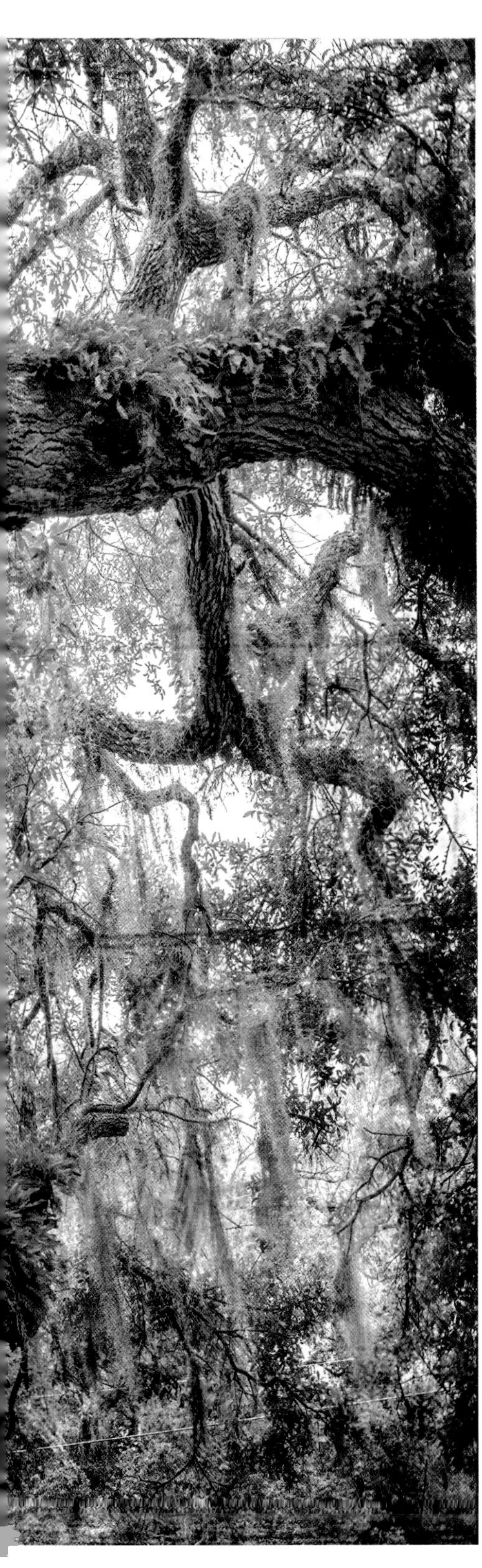

TREE BESIDE FORMER FERRY HOUSE, ROCKVILLE
A twisting tree grows alongside a two-story dwelling that was a ferry house on the Inner Passage in the late 1700s and 1800s.

MCLEOD OAK, JAMES ISLAND
This live oak tree, estimated to be between 300 and 600 years old, stands between former slave dwellings and cotton fields. McLeod Plantation's crop was loaded onto wooden boats that carried the cotton to market on the Inner Passage.

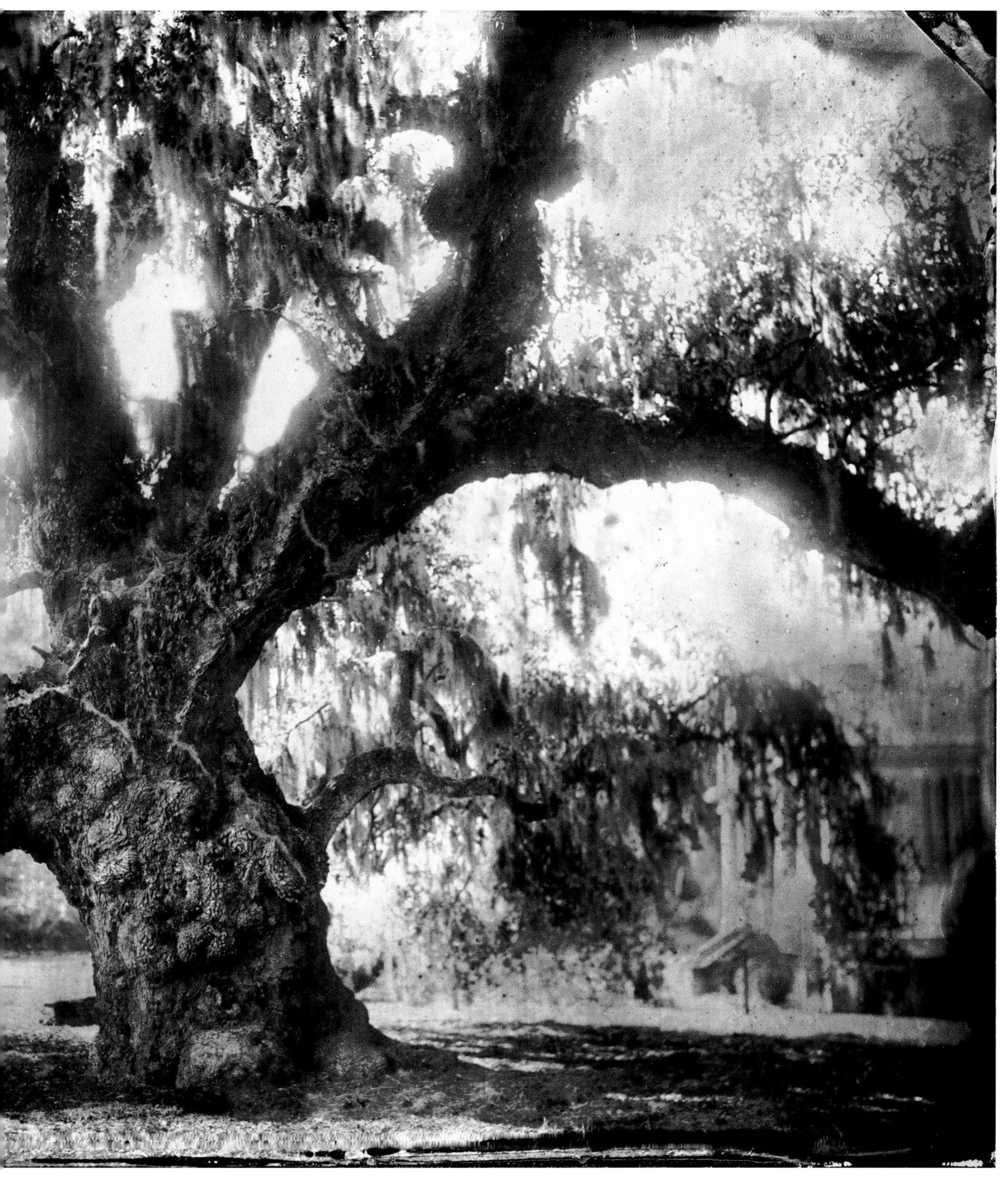

SWIMMING IN HISTORY AT NEW CUT CANAL

VIRGINIA MCGEE RICHARDS

I didn't intend to spend ten years searching for one man's name.

My obsession began in a tidal creek where I went to swim in South Carolina. It was the summer I was pregnant with my fourth child and I longed for a quiet escape from Charleston's tourist-swarmed streets. Behind Wadmalaw Island, I found a place where I could slip down a mud embankment and lower myself into a canal called New Cut. I became a suspended bather, swimming through water so rich with silt that I couldn't see below the surface. In this forgotten corner of the Lowcountry, the loudest noise was the chattering and clicking of shrimp singing beneath the surface. As I floated back and forth with the sea tide, I wondered about the canal's origins. The British colonial name of New Cut was different from other nearby creeks—Wadmalaw, Bohicket, Leadenwah, Stono—all named in Indigenous dialects.

Naively, I thought that discovering New Cut's origin story wouldn't require much research grit—especially in Charleston, South Carolina, where history is worshipped. Charleston is filled with libraries and special rooms dedicated to preserving the past in carefully curated collections of diaries, maps, ledgers, and colonial archives. To investigate New Cut, I intended to swing by the local library, look through an index and read a couple of paragraphs about my swimming hole.

But there was no written history of New Cut anywhere.

Librarians advised that few historical records from the area around New Cut had survived centuries of weather, a county courthouse fire, and war. During the Civil War, South Carolina transferred official papers from the Lowcountry, where New Cut is located, to Columbia for safe keeping. Many paper records were burned when General Sherman's army marched across the state in 1865. A local historian in the Charleston Public Library pointed me toward the bookshelf where French and British maps were kept and suggested that I look there for New Cut's origins.

The absence of a written history hooked me, and my quick trip to the library became a quest. Burning through days that became years in windowless archives, I fed reels of microfilm through a reader and combed through faded documents. Only after thousands of hours of research did I begin to weave together the story of New Cut canal. The few historical documents that I found revealed that my swimming hole at New Cut had been carved from the earth by enslaved Black men. Thumbing through a compendium of old drawings, my first real clue to the canal's origins was marked on a rare map from 1711.[1] On the map, a surveyor had written "The Cutt" for "New Cut" in the place where I wade into the creek to swim.[2]

Using the date 1711, I went back in time to the late 1600s and early 1700s to learn that enslaved and indentured men were forced to build New Cut, a mile-long watery traverse through a dense cypress forest. The work required felling primeval trees measuring six feet in diameter and digging a deep trench through the marsh to accommodate boat traffic.[3] During construction, Black men shoveled mud through malarial swamps, while battling snakes and alligators in intense heat. Once created, New Cut allowed colonial travelers to rely on strong sea tides to carry them through the canal.

In the 1700s when the canals of the Inner Passage—New Cut, Haulover Cut, New Town Cut, Wappoo Cut, and Elliott's Cut—were constructed, Black workers were listed as itemized property. These individuals shaped Charleston's politics and economy by building canals, roads, bridges, forts—virtually all the colony's infrastructure—but their contributions were not documented and their names are unknown. Their work, however, has survived in the deep trenches at New Cut which have endured for three hundred years. These six-foot walls of mud engineered to hold tidal water still stand just below the water's surface.

British plans for a canal system through the Lowcountry were ambitious, and New Cut was only one of dozens of hand-dug waterways. By 1750, enslaved men had constructed a reliable water route extending over three hundred miles from Charleston, South Carolina, to St. Augustine, Florida. This inland route, protected from sea storms and pirates, enabled travelers to journey safely up and down the coast as if on a modern interstate highway. Colonists called the corridor "The Inner Passage" or "The Way Southward."

Enslaved and indentured people in Carolina used the Inner Passage for their own ends. Subverting Britain's original intent for the canal system, freedom seekers used the water passage as a route to flee from the colony.

1 Edward Crisp, "A Compleat Description of the Province of Carolina in 3 Parts. 1st. The Improved Part from the Surveys of Maurice Mathews & Mr. John Love. 2ly. The West Part by Capt. Tho. Nairn. 3ly: A Chart of the Coast from Virginia to Cape Florida," 1711, US Library of Congress, accessed January 14, 2025, https://www.loc.gov/resource/g3870.ct001123/?r=0.338,0.307,0.343,0.214,0.

2 Nic Butler, "The 'Crisp Map' of 1711," *Rediscovering Charleston's Colonial Fortifications: A Weblog for the Mayor's "Walled City" Task Force* (blog), April 17, 2008, https://walledcitytaskforce.org/2008/04/17/crisp-map/.

3 Maurice Mathews, "A Contemporary View," *South Carolina Historical Magazine* 55, no. 3 (July 1954): 155; "Extract of a Letter from Benjamin Reynolds, Esq. to the Author, Dated Wadmalaw, December 1, 1808," in David Ramsay, *History of South Carolina*, vol. 2 (1858; repr., London: FB &c Ltd, 2018), 155, 187.

Over a century before the advent of the Underground Railroad to the north, enslaved Carolinians planned and carried out their own escapes by paddling three hundred miles southward on the Inner Passage.[4] Once they reached a Spanish fort at St. Augustine, the Spanish governor freed them if they agreed to convert to Catholicism. Some of these refugees' expeditions are memorialized in escaped slave notices in a colonial newspaper, the *South Carolina Gazette*. In 1732, "two Negro Women, one named Delia, having with a sucking Child, and she speaks very little English; and the other named Clarinda" escaped on the waterway in a "Cyprus Canoe about 25 Foot long and 3 Foot wide."[5] While some escapees traveled all the way to St. Augustine, others navigated canoes into uncharted swamps such as those near New Cut to join maroon communities formed by runaway slaves.[6]

4 J. G. Dunlop, "William Dunlop's Mission to St. Augustine in 1698," *South Carolina Historical and Genealogical Magazine* (January 1933).

5 Escaped slave notices, *South Carolina Gazette*, June 17, 1732.

6 Timothy J. Lockley, ed., *Maroon Communities in South Carolina* (Columbia: University of South Carolina Press, 2009), 14, 19, 31, 57.

Today it's possible to experience the Inner Passage by taking a short boat ride southward from Charleston to Kiawah Island. Luxury yachters, kayakers, and recreational fishermen routinely navigate these waterways without knowing their connection to enslavement. To the casual visitor, New Cut Canal appears to be just another peaceful creek, a place where a Charleston resident can cool off and play. But, during my escapes to the water at New Cut, I now know I had been swimming in history. The canals are receding back into native grasslands. Haulover Cut has already fragmented into an unrecognizable jumble of marsh and hammocks behind Kiawah Island. Evidence of the canals and the Inner Passage is rapidly disappearing along with the legacy of the people who built them.

As I walked the canal routes along the coast, I learned to appreciate how easy it is to become disoriented in this watery landscape of undisturbed marsh grass and water extending for miles in all directions. The marsh's base layer is a heavy dark muck known to locals as "pluff mud." It is otherworldly: a dark gray glue that pulls off your boot or consumes your whole leg with one misstep. In the blasting afternoon sun, the stench of fermenting earth and decay steams off the marsh. Every hour, this muddy landscape changes as steady tides fill creeks and low basins with seven feet of ocean surge.

A constant in the coastal swamps is the giant heritage trees—live oaks that have lived for hundreds of years along the banks of the Inner Passage. Some of the oldest trees are named, like the "Angel Oak," a centuries-old tree standing in a churchyard. There is something magical about the trees—tourists travel miles to stand under their twisted boughs. Protected by twenty-four-hour surveillance and an eight-foot fence, the Angel Oak draws four hundred thousand visitors each year.

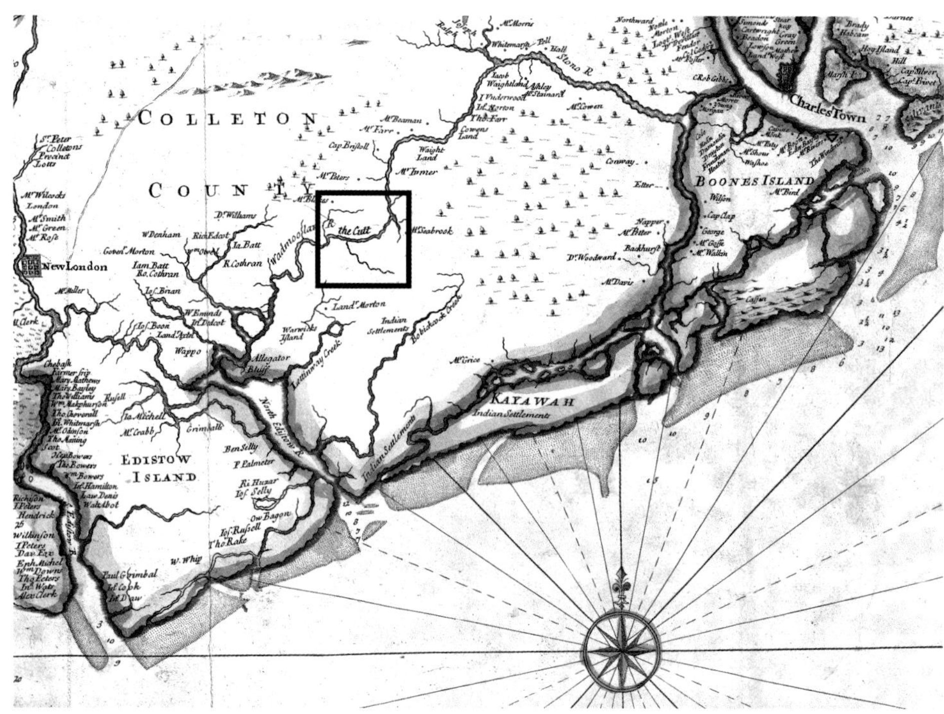

SECTION OF 1711 EDWARD CRISP MAP, "A COMPLEAT DESCRIPTION OF THE PROVINCE OF CAROLINA IN 3 PARTS."

Over hundreds of years, oaks growing along the Inner Passage absorbed the sight of angled elbows against the land, backs bent, as hundreds of men sacrificed their lives to carve canals from the swamp. The trees stood over Black men burrowing so deeply into the gray marsh that they disappeared into it. There may be no documents in the libraries, but the trees hold bits and shards of this land's collective memory. The heritage oaks are the last living witnesses to the history of the Inner Passage.

I became a pilgrim at New Cut, returning to walk, and to swim, and to photograph for over a decade in search of clues to the canal's history. Determined to find the most telling viewpoints, I explored the waterways by foot, boat, and plane. To create the aerial image of the Stono River, I leaned out the window of a 1960s press plane and photographed with my digital camera. The digital file was then converted to a "positive" image on slide film. In the darkroom, an enlarger projected the positive slide onto a glass plate coated with collodion and silver nitrate.

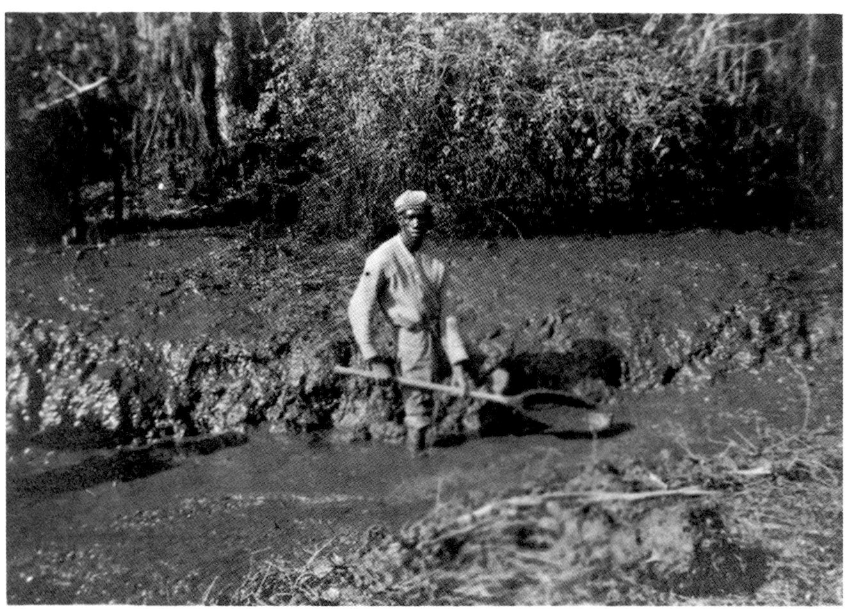

DIGGING A CANAL WITH A WOODEN SHOVEL AT MULBERRY PLANTATION, CHARLESTON, SOUTH CAROLINA, 1916. (Photograph courtesy of Historic Charleston Foundation Archives)

My hope is that images can convey a landscape scarred with secrets, where on rare mornings an ethereal mist rises off fields to meet the certainty of past violence held by the soil. Planting seasons, river baptisms, torture, prayers, African dialects, poverty, massacres, lynchings. The land remembers but cannot speak. By documenting the Inner Passage, I want to give the land a voice.

ENSLAVED AND INDENTURED PEOPLE ESCAPING IN BOATS ON THE INNER PASSAGE

1671 Dennis Mahoon
John Rivers
John Cooke
1672 John Radcliffe
William Davys
Richard Gardiner
1672 Richard Hicklin
John Rivers
1687 Conano
Jesse
Jaque
Gran Domingo
Cambo
Mingo
Dique
Robi
two women
one girl-child
1697 Divers Runaway Slaves
Cyrus
1717 Several Servts
1724 Sam
Jamie
Boatswain
Coffey
Coffey branded H. T. on the right Shoulder
1724 Sabina
two year old child
Sarah
London
Hector Markt with: the letter P in his forehead
Augustine
1725 Escaped slave from Carolina
1725 23 Negroes belonging to John Bull and others
1725 a large Canoe with several others, but that they were drowned
1725 James Allen
London Jeffers
Botayan Marriner
Robert Pilaot
Samuell Seauseau
Coffee Stone
Coffee Thomas
1732 Jack
Hercules
Monday
Amoretta
Sarah
1732 Delia with sucking Child
Clarinda
1733 William Merick
Mullarey Gill
1733 James Hewitt
Holemark
1734 Hector
Peter
Dublin
1734 Francis Burn
1735 Charles
1737 Steven
1737 John Seeker
John Watsone
1738 Canoe going by, wherein were three runaway Negroes from Carolina
1738 nineteen Negroes and five others ran away from Port Royal and successfully made it to St. Augustine

1739 Jace
Will
1739 Billy
Adam
Fortune
1739 Caesar
Allchoy
1741 a Spaniard
a young Negro Boy, of thin Visage
1742 Casar
1743 Richard Edwards
Henry Jarvis
Michael Miller
William Thompson
an old Woman
her daughter
September 1743 two Negroes near Savannah caught in a Small Boat making their Escape from their Master in Carolina
1744 Negro Fellow
1744 Three Negro Men
Negro Fellow taken up at Stono
1744 two Runaway Negroes from Carolina
1746 Chamberlain, having been use to go in a Pettianugs
1746 two Negro Men, a new Cypres Canow, about 20 Feet long, and 3 Feet and 10 Inches wide, rows with 4 Oars, parpentin'd without and within

1748 James Hale
Thomas Eddy
Mark Matthews
John Jenkins
1748 Moses his Country Name Monvigo . . .
Sampson
June 1749 Six Negroes belonging to Mr. Joseph Butler and one belonging to Mrs. Sarah Woodward ran away with boat belonging to Mr. Alexander McPherson
1749 group of Negroes stole a large Canoe and were seen on the Way to the Southward
October 23, 1749 21 Negroes at Port-Royal went off from thence in a boat they stole
1749 Casar
1749 Cato Assisting in Stealing a Boat and sundry goods and running away to St. Augustine
1751 London
Hereford
1752 Paul
Issac
1754 Quacee
1758 a short, well-set Angela Negro Man, branded on one Shoulder T.W.
1758 Jack
Galway
Fortune
Samson
One Negro Wench
Dabar
Sabina
Rabel
one negro boy named They
1761 negro goes by the names of Nantz, Lance, and Anson
1761 some runaway negroes, at Mr. Rantowle's point
1761 Christopher in an iron with three prongs on one of his legs
1761 Peter having procured a Boat, Arms, Ammunition and provisions and therewith attempted to Go to St. Augustine
1762 Crack
free Indian Wench, wife to the fellow Crack
child about two years of age
his mother Pegg
Harry
white man

1762 two run away negroes
1763 Alice
1765 George
1766 some run-away Negroes
1767 Cupid
1767 Tom
1767 Some run-away Negroes
1767 Cato
1768 John
1768 Tom
Peter
Pompey
Arabella
Castilla (son)
1769 . . . carried off with them a good many cloaths, three blankets, and two hats, and went off in a canoe belonging to Mr. John Holmes, the canoe rows with four oars, and has been new bottomed with two cypress planks joining together, her upper rudder iron goes across her stern . . .
Boston
Toney
Marcellus
1772 . . . small CYPRESS CANOW, about Fourteen and Half Feet long, and Three and One-Fourteen Feet wide, marked with brown Paint on the out-Side of her Stern, something resembling thus and having a small Fourteen Feet long Chain and Staple, at her Head . . .
Negro Man
1772 . . . a small YAWL, about 12 or 13 Feet-long, and between 4 and 5 Feet wide, has two Ring bolts, the one in the Head, and the other in the Stern, rows with three Oars, and is made for one Sail forward . . .
Negro, supposed to be Run-away
1772 . . . open Boat . . .
Monday
1772 . . . small CYPRESS CANOE, about 15 feet long, and about 2 feet 3 inches wide, with a piece put in her head, and having a small chain about 7 feet long, with a staple in her head, and a small padlock . . .
2 negro men, supposed to be run-away
1773 Will
1773 Saul
Jack
They are both stout well-made Fellows, and had heavy Irons on their Legs when they went away . . . They were formerly Free, and are well known in Georgia by the Names of Saul and John Winners. They were born in Bermuda . . .
1775 . . . went off from Wando this Day in a Schooner's Canoe . . .
Bob
Bill
Billy
1787 Lewis
Chicheum
Peter
Dembo
Cupid
Fortune
Betty
Juliett
Peggy
Little Coke
Frank
Dick
Joe
Sharper called Captain Cudjoe
Jemmy
Joe

1800 Cyrus
Hercules
Tom
1821 Jack
Joe called Forest
Wife of Joe
Mistress of Joe
Anderson
wife of Anderson
three-year old child
Isam
Stephon
1824–1826 Will
Newton
1825 Jemmy
Adam
Keating
Eleck
Owen
John
Issac
Susey
Dolly
Chloe
Chloe
5 children
No Date Mowby
Dunmore

SOURCES

The names, dates, and descriptions listed above are sourced from colonial newspapers and archival references in treatises. Each separate date represents one boat of freedom seekers. In some cases, colonial records do not identify escapees by name, only by their attributes. Descriptive words included in this list of people are copied verbatim from the archival record. Further information can be found in the sources listed below.

Charleston Courier. "200 Dollars Reward." Runaway slave advertisement, May 28, 1825.

Duncan, John Donald. *Servitude and Slavery in Colonial South Carolina 1670–1776*, Part 2. Ann Arbor, MI: Published on demand by University Microfilms 1972. [1717 boat] 618, [1671 boat and 1672 boat] 636–637, [1697 boat] 645, [1716 boat] 648, [1724 boats and 1725 boats] 651–654, [1738 boat] 661, [1739 boat] 668, [1743 boat and 1744 boat] 673, [1749 boat] 674, [1749 boats] 675, [1749 boat] 676, [1749 boat] 678, [1749 boat, 1761 boats] 680–681.

Dunlop, J. G. "William Dunlop's Mission to St. Augustine in 1688." *South Carolina Historical and Genealogical Magazine* 34, no. 1 (1933): [1687 boat] 26.

Lockley, Timothy James. *Maroon Communities in South Carolina: A Documentary Record.* Columbia: University of South Carolina Press, 2009. [1787 boat] 63–65, [1800 boat] 73, [1821 boat] 95–112, [1824–1826 boat] 121.

South Carolina Gazette. Escaped slave notices: May 6, 1732; June 17, 1732; April 14, 1733; August 4, 1733; February 9, 1734; June 21, 1735; January 22, 1737; February 26, 1737; March 17, 1739; September 18, 1741; November 21, 1743; June 11, 1744; November 26, 1744; May 19, 1746; July 20, 1746; August 3, 1746; April 18, 1748; April 27, 1748; May 2, 1748; January 19, 1749; June 24, 1751; August 1, 1754; October 6, 1758; October 13, 1758; December 15, 1758; April 25, 1761; May 2, 1761; May 9, 1761; October 3, 1761; February 20, 1762; February 27, 1762; March 6, 1762; March 13, 1762; March 20, 1762; March 28, 1762; June 4, 1763; July 15, 1765; May 6, 1766; January 12, 1767; January 13, 1767; July 27, 1767; December 22, 1767; December 29, 1767; January 19, 1768; January 26, 1768; February 2, 1768; March 1, 1768; March 8, 1768; March 15, 1768; June 27, 1768; August 8, 1769; August 15, 1769; January 21, 1772; February 11, 1772; May 7, 1772; May 19, 1772; January 28, 1773; August 23, 1773; September 6, 1773; September 15, 1773; November 10, 1775.

ACKNOWLEDGMENTS

This book is dedicated to the Carolinians whose stories inspired me to begin documenting Lowcountry waterways. I am indebted to Carrie and Bill Griffin and Hugh and Charles Lane, all of whom allowed me to roam their land on the Inner Passage route for several years.

Many people have supported this project from the beginning. Over a decade ago, Elizabeth Daniel encouraged me to discover the story of the South Carolina canals. Historian Nic Butler met me on my first visit to the Charleston Public Library and continued to supply source materials. Charlestonian and author Rutledge Hammes encouraged the project as I studied maps on my kitchen floor. Photographer Lisa Elmaleh braved all the biting insects in South Carolina to help process plates in the field. Joann Sieburg-Baker challenged me to see the landscapes of the Inner Passage as a visual poem. My family, in particular Grace, Clara, and Carson, edited texts and reviewed images for this book. I recall waiting for the first minutes of daylight to walk marshes with native Charlestonians Jane Maybank and Kathleen Saunders. I am also thankful for my agent, Joan Brookbank, who has remained steadfast through all the challenges of the bookmaking process and introduced me to Victoria Hindley of the MIT Press, who embraced this project. I would also like to thank Anita Lewin of Singer Editions for her amazing eye and expert advice.

The Inner Passage project would not have been possible without the mentorship of photographers James Estrin and Ed Kashi, both of whom critiqued and encouraged my photography through the Anderson Ranch Visual Arts Center. Working with historian and author Dr. Peter H. Wood has been a privilege and an honor. He is always curious about new historical interpretations.

Appreciation also is extended to the following organizations that allowed access to their properties for exploring and photographing:

The Charleston Museum
Georgetown Rice Museum
Brick House Ruins Preservation
Middleburg Plantation
Charleston County Parks and Recreation Commission

BIBLIOGRAPHY

Butler, Nic. "The 'Crisp Map' of 1711." *Rediscovering Charleston's Colonial Fortifications: A Weblog for the Mayor's "Walled City" Task Force* (blog), April 17, 2008. https://walledcitytaskforce.org/2008/04/17/crisp-map/.

Catesby, Mark. "Mark Catesby's Natural History." Excerpted in *The Colonial South Carolina Scene: Contemporary Views, 1697–1774*, edited by H. Roy Merrens. Columbia: University of South Carolina Press, 1977.

Crisp, Edward. *A Compleat Description of the Province of Carolina in 3 Parts. 1st. The Improved Part from the Surveys of Maurice Mathews & Mr. John Love. 2ly. The West Part by Capt. Tho. Nairn. 3ly: A Chart of the Coast from Virginia to Cape Florida.* 82 x 99 cm. London, 1711. US Library of Congress. https://www.loc.gov/resource/g3870.ct001123/?r=0.338,0.307,0.343,0.214,0.

Deas Moore, Vennie, with William P. Baldwin. *The Fishermen of the Lowcountry: Memories from Home.* Mount Pleasant, SC: Arcadia Press, 2007.

Drayton, John. *A View of South Carolina, As Respects Her Natural and Civil Concerns.* Charleston, SC: W. P. Young, 1802.

Dunlop, J. G. "William Dunlop's Mission to St. Augustine in 1688." *South Carolina Historical and Genealogical Magazine* 34, no. 1 (1933). https://www.jstor.org/stable/27571354.

Ferebee, L. R. *A Brief History of the Slave Life of Rev. L. R. Ferebee, and the Battles of Life, and Four Years of His Ministerial Life: Written from Memory. To 1882.* Edwards, Broughton & Co., 1882.

Harris, Lynn. *Patroons and Periaguas: Enslaved Watermen and Watercraft of the Lowcountry.* Columbia: University of South Carolina Press, 2014.

Jones, George Fenwick. "John Martin Boltzius' Trip to Charleston, October 1742." *South Carolina Historical Magazine* 82, no. 2 (1981): 92. https://www.jstor.org/stable/27567679.

Landers, Jane. *Black Society in Spanish Florida.* Champaign: University of Illinois Press, 1999.

Landers, Jane. "'Giving Liberty to All': Spanish Florida as a Black Sanctuary, 1693–1770." In *La Florida: Five Hundred Years of Hispanic Presence*, edited by Viviana Díaz Balsera and Rachel A. May. Gainesville: University Press of Florida, 2014.

Lipscomb, Terry W., ed. *The Journal of the Commons House of Assembly: Nov. 21, 1752–Sept. 6, 1754*. Columbia: University of South Carolina Press, 1983.

Lockley, Timothy J., ed. *Maroon Communities in South Carolina*. Columbia: University of South Carolina Press, 2009.

Mathews, Maurice. "A Contemporary View of Carolina in 1680." *South Carolina Historical Magazine* 55, no. 3 (1954): 155. https://www.jstor.org/stable/i27563604.

McCord, David J., ed. "Containing the Acts Relating to Roads, Bridges and Ferries." In *Statutes at Large of South Carolina*, vol. 9. Columbia, SC: A. S. Johnston Press, 1841.

McGill, Joseph, Jr. and Herb Frazier. *Sleeping with the Ancestors: How I Followed the Footprints of Slavery*. New York: Grand Central Publishing, 2023.

Merrens, H. Roy, ed. *The Colonial South Carolina Scene: Contemporary Views, 1697–1774*. Columbia: University of South Carolina Press, 1977.

Ramsay, David. *History of South Carolina: From Its First Settlement in 1670 to the Year 1808*. Vol. 2. 1858; repr., London: FB &c Ltd, 2018.

Salley, Alexander, ed. "Journal of Elder William Pratt, 1695–1701." In *Early Narratives of Carolina, 1650–1708*. New York: Charles Scribner's Sons, 1911.

Salley, A. S., ed. *Journals of the Commons House of Assembly of South Carolina for 1702*. Columbia, SC, 1916.

Seutter, George Matthaeus, cartographer. *Plan Von Neu Ebenezer*. 1747. Black-and-white line engraving with period hand-color on laid paper. Accessed on January 15, 2025. https://emuseum.history.org/objects/31214/plan-von-neu-ebenezer.

Wood, Peter H. *Black Majority: Race, Rice, and Rebellion in South Carolina, 1670–1740*. New York: W. W. Norton, 2024.

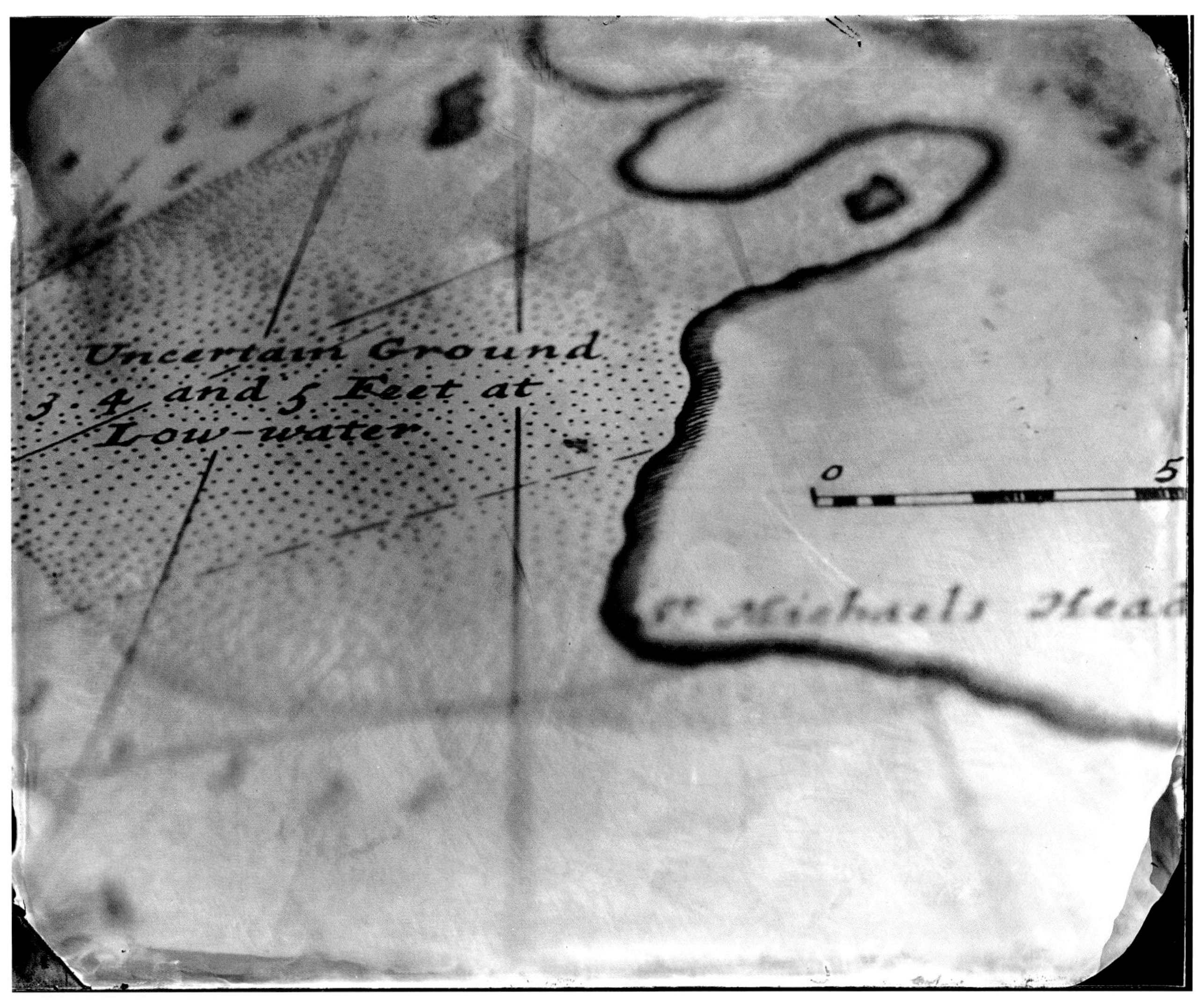

CLOSE-UP OF MAP BY HERMAN MOLL, CIRCA 1711
Archival map showing "Uncertain Ground" and "Low-water" in the harbor at Port Royal, a town located on the waterway south of Charleston that was settled in the early 1700s.